SIGNS

of the
TRUE
CHURCH
of
CHRIST

Michael T. Griffith

ISBN: 0-88290-337-3
Horizon Publishers' Catalog and Order Number: 1034
First Printing: February, 1989

Printing: 2 3 4 5 6 7 8 9 10

Printed and distributed
in the United States of America by

Horizon
Publishers
& Distributors, Incorporated
P.O. Box 490 Bountiful, Utah 84010-0490

About The Author

Michael T. Griffith joined the LDS Church in 1977 at the age of nineteen. Ever since his conversion, he has been an avid student of Mormon studies and ancient history.

Brother Griffith served a mission in the Texas Dallas Mission. During his mission he developed a program on Book of Mormon evidences which was presented several times during his missionary labors. After leaving the mission field Brother Griffith attended Ricks Jr. College and then Brigham Young University, where his studies centered around ancient history.

At BYU he worked as an assistant to the head of the Society for Early Historic Archaeology (SEHA). In 1982 that organization published his paper on the famous Lehi Tree-of-Life Stone, *The Lehi Tree-of-Life Story in the Book of Mormon Still Supported By Izapa Stela 5.*

In 1983 Brother Griffith graduated in Modern Standard Arabic and Egyptian dialect from the DLI-Foreign Language Center in Monterey, California. In 1987 he graduated in Hebrew from the same institution.

Brother Griffith has held several Church callings, including ward clerk, Sunday School and Primary teacher, and ward newsletter editor. He is married to the former Rosemarie Lynn Pratt and they are the parents of four children.

Table of Contents

Introduction

The Church of Jesus Christ of Latter-day Saints (often referred to as the Mormon Church) claims to be a restoration of the same church which was organized anciently by Christ and His apostles.

A powerful evidence for this claim is the striking resemblance between the Mormon church of today and Christ's ancient church. This book points out many of the doctrinal beliefs in which that resemblance is apparent.

Latter-day Saint missionaries often ask this question to non-members whom they are visiting, "If Jesus Christ were to restore the same church He organized in New Testament times, with apostles, prophets, revelation, miracles, and all the rest, would you want to join it?" Most people will immediately answer, "Yes!"

This is the challenge that Latter-day Saints offer to the world: we proclaim that The Church of Jesus Christ of Latter-day Saints *is* the Savior's true church restored to the earth.

The Lord brought about this restoration through a latter-day prophet, Joseph Smith. In 1820 God the Father and the Lord Jesus Christ appeared to him in answer to his sincere inquiry as to which church he should join. Young Joseph was told that he should join none of the existing churches, and he learned that the true church would soon be restored through him. The promised restoration came to pass, and in 1830 the Mormon church was officially and lawfully organized.

In recent decades modern Biblical and historical scholarship has clarified and expanded man's understanding of the ancient Christian church. In doing so, it has also provided numerous evidences for the truthfulness of Mormonism. For example, there is now very strong evidence (in addition to the Biblical witness) that such uniquely Mormon teachings as man's pre-mortal existence and his potential of deification were firmly held doctrines of the early church.

If any church today claims to be the true church of Jesus Christ, the validity of its claim can be established or rejected by comparing it to these principles. The honest seeker after truth will discover, as I did, that only The Church of Jesus Christ of Latter-day Saints possesses all of these traits today.

This book has been prepared as a brief study and reference guide for those desiring to learn more about the essential doctrine and practices of the Lord's church in ancient times.

My objective has been to be brief, while listing sources which will be rewarding to those students who examine them. This is, indeed, a study guide, not an exhaustive treatise.

Although some of the signs are supported by both scriptural references and historical quotations, the quotes do not constitute all or even a majority of the evidence for those signs. To examine further evidence for a particular sign, one should examine all of the references given in the "References for Further Study" section for that sign.

1

The Godhead: Three Separate Beings

Essential Doctrine:

According to the Bible and other ancient Christian and Jewish sources, any church claiming to be the true Church of Jesus Christ **must believe that the Godhead is composed of three separate and distinct deities: God the Father, the Lord Jesus Christ, and the Holy Ghost.**

Key Bible Passages:

Matt. 3:16-17	When Jesus is baptized, the Spirit of God descends on him like a dove, and a voice from heaven calls him my beloved Son.
Matt. 12:31-32	Words spoken against Jesus may be forgiven, but blasphemy against the Holy Ghost shall not be forgiven.
Matt. 18:10	In heaven their angels do always behold the face of my Father which is in heaven.
Matt. 26:39-42	O my Father, not as I will, but as thou wilt; thy will be done.
Matt. 28:19	Go teach all nations, baptizing them in the name of the Father, and of the Son, and of the Holy Ghost.

Mark 1:10-22	Jesus comes out of the water, the Spirit like a dove descends upon him, and a voice from heaven calls him my beloved Son.
Luke 3:21-23	When Jesus is baptized, the Holy Ghost descends in the shape of a dove, and a voice from heaven calls him my beloved Son.
John 3:5	Jesus says, unless a man be born of the Spirit, he cannot enter into the kingdom of God.
John 14:26	The Father will send the Holy Ghost in Christ's name.
John 20:17	I ascend unto my Father, and your Father, and to my God, and your God.
Acts 2:33	Christ is exalted on the right hand of God by the promise of the Holy Ghost.
Acts 7:55-56	Stephen, full of the Holy Ghost, looks up and sees Jesus standing on the right hand of God.
2 Cor. 13:14	The grace of Christ, the love of God, and the communion of the Holy Ghost be with you all.
1 John 5:7	There are three that bear record in heaven, the Father, the Word, and the Holy Ghost.

References for Further Study:

1. James E. Talmage, *The Articles of Faith* (Salt Lake City, Utah: The Church of Jesus Christ of Latter-day Saints, 1976), pp. 29-51.

2. Keith Norman, "Ex Nihilo: The Development of the Doctrines of God and Creation in Early Christianity," *BYU Studies* (Spring, 1977), pp. 291-318.

3. See also sections 2, 3, 4, 5, 6 and 8 of this book.

2

Father Above Son, United in Purpose

Essential Doctrine:

According to the Bible and other ancient Christian and Jewish sources, any church claiming to be the true Church of Jesus Christ must believe that **God the Son, Jesus Christ has power equal to God the Father, but is subordinate to Father because of his divine sonship and personal obedience and love. They are united in purpose, but are separate individuals.**

Key Bible Passages:

The Divine Sonship of Jesus Christ

Matt. 3:17 (16-17)	This is my beloved Son, in whom I am well pleased.
Matt. 16:16 (13-17)	Thou are the Christ, the Son of the living God.
Matt. 17:5 (1-9)	This is my beloved Son, in whom I am well pleased.
Matt. 27:43	He trusted in God, for he said, I am the Son of God.
Luke 1:32 (28-38)	He shall be called the Son of the Highest: and the Lord God shall give unto him the throne of David.

John 1:14 (1-14)	We beheld His glory, as of the only begotten of the Father.

The Relationship of Jesus Christ to God the Father

Luke 23:35	Christ, the chosen of God.
John 1:1 (1-3)	The Word was with God, and the Word was God.
John 5:18 (17-20)	Christ said God was his Father, making himself equal with God.
John 5:19 (17-20)	The Son can do nothing of himself, but what he seeth the Father do.
John 5:20 (17-22)	The Father loveth the Son, and sheweth him all things that himself doeth.
John 8:28 (28-29)	I do nothing of myself; but as my Father hath taught me.
John 8:29 (28-29)	The Father hath not left me alone; for I do always those things that please him.
John 10:15 (14-15)	As the Father knoweth me, even so know I the Father.
John 14:28 (28-31)	I go unto the Father: for my Father is greater than I.
John 17:7 (1-18)	All things whatsoever thou hast given me are of thee.
Acts 7:55 (54-56)	Stephen saw Jesus standing on the right hand of God.
1 Cor. 1:24	Christ the power of God, and the wisdom of God.
1 Cor. 11:3	The head of Christ is God.
1 Cor. 15:28 (24-28)	Then shall the Son also himself be subject unto him that put all things under him, that God may be all in all.
2 Cor. 4:6 (3-6)	God gives the glory of God in the face of Jesus Christ.
Eph. 1:17	The God of our Lord Jesus Christ, the Father of glory.

Philip. 2:6 (5-11)	Christ thought it not robbery to be equal with God.
Col. 1:19 (13-19)	It pleased the Father that in him (Christ) should all fulness dwell.
Col. 2:9 (8-11)	In him (Christ) dwelleth all the fulness of the Godhead bodily.
Heb. 1:2 (1-14)	God hath spoken by his Son, whom he hath appointed heir of all things, by whom also he made the worlds.
1 Jn 2:1 (1-2)	We have an advocate with the Father, Jesus Christ the righteous.

References for Further Study:

1. See sections 1, 3, 4, 5, 6 and 8 of this book.

Explanatory Notes:

Howard Clark Kee, a former instructor of Religious Thought at the University of Pennsylvania, and later a professor of New Testament studies at Drew University's Theological School, wrote:

> John says unequivocally that the Word of God...was made flesh in Jesus of Nazareth....He [John] is careful to point out that God and the Word are not interchangeable terms. Rather, the Word possesses the essential qualities of God,...
>
> But wherein lies the unity of the Father and the Son? It is by no means a matter of simple identity, as though Jesus was God the Father in disguise. The Son utters the words of God (ch. 3:34); he does what he sees the Father doing (ch. 5:29). Because he claims to be working God's works in his healing ministry, "the Jews" accuse him of making himself equal with God (v. 18). The Father has committed all judgement to the Son, and has

given him the power to give life (vs. 21-22). The Son is the supreme object of the Father's love, and honor and obedience to the Son are tantamount to honor and obedience to the Father. The son comes in the authority of the Father (vs. 43) and his works bear witness that the Father has sent him (vs. 36). What the Son declares to the world is what he has heard from God....The oneness of Jesus with God is a unity of works, of will, of devotion, of obedience by which Jesus is uniquely the instrument of God's purpose to disclose his nature and create his people.

Another unity for which John is concerned is the unity of the people of God. The people of God bear the same relationship to Jesus Christ that he bears to God the Father. As God sent Christ, so Christ sends forth his people (ch. 17:18). As the Father gave his word to the Son, so the Son gives God's word to his people (vs. 8, 14). The glory that God gave to Jesus Christ he has given to them; the love with which God loved him he has poured out upon them (vs. 22-23). (Howard Clark Kee, *Jesus and God's New People* (Philadelphia, Pennsylvania: The Westminster Press, 1959), pp. 89-91.)

As Kee states above, although Jesus and the Father are one in purpose they are not the same person. When the Savior said that "I and my Father are one" (John 10:30), He was simply saying that He and the Father are one in purpose. Jesus prayed that His disciples would be one in the same way that He and the Father are one. (John 17:5-22.) This oneness was clearly one of works, will, and devotion—nothing more, nothing less. Obviously, Jesus was not the Father in disguise. He was in "the express image" of His Father, and He obeyed the Father in all things. He was the perfect representative of the Father. Thus, in John 14:9 Jesus could say in all truthfulness that he who had seen Him had seen the Father. But this verse does not mean that Jesus and the Father are the same person. The New Testament makes it crystal clear in dozens of places that Jesus and the Father are two separate and distinct beings.

Richard Lloyd Anderson, a professor of Greek and New Testament studies at Brigham Young University, has said the following about the oneness of the Father and the Son:

> As Paul explained his relationship with Apollos, he said they were co-workers on the same building, God's temple or Church. He added the image of farming: "I have planted, Apollos watered; but God gave the increase" (1 Cor. 3:6). Thus "he who plants and he who waters are one" (1 Cor. 3:8, New King James Bible [NKJB]), a verbal construction identical to Jesus' language, "I and my Father are one" (John 10:30). [In both verses the Greek word for "one" is "hen."]
>
> There is no more biblical reason for merging the Father and Son than for thinking that Paul and Apollos physically merged. In his prayer for unity,...Jesus equated the oneness of believers with the oneness of the Father and the Son. And at the end of 1 Corinthians, Paul teaches the glorious resurrection of individuals; so, like believers, the Father and the Son exist in glory now as individuals. Otherwise Paul could not sensibly close his plea for unity with the verbal separation of the Father and Son: "and ye are Christ's; and Christ is God's" (1 Cor. 3:23)....
>
> Paul opens Hebrews with the Father sending the Son, who is the "brightness of his glory, and the *express image* of his person" (Heb. 1:3, italics added). The italicized words

translate the Greek "charakter," the ancestor of the English "character," which roughly approximates Paul's meaning.

Christ is the "character" of God's being, the apostle says. This term meant the "mark" of an engraving tool—in physical terms a "stamped likeness" or "an exact reproduction." Thus, Christ is not the Father, but he is stamped with his [the Father's] divinity and exact form. And this is not in some mystic sense of sharing the same soul, for man in his distinctiveness from God is also said to be in God's "character" in early Christian literature. Clement of Rome [an early Christian bishop] wrote about A.D. 96 and said that God formed man in the "likeness of his own image." [Cf. Genesis 1:26-27; 5:1,3.] In the opening of Hebrews Christ is clearly distinct from God, standing "on the right hand of the Majesty on high" (Heb. 1:3)....

Romans testified that Christ was "at the right hand of God" making "intercession for us" (Romans 8:34; also vs. 27). And Hebrews unfolds the Atonement with the same picture of the Lord "on the right hand of the throne of the Majesty" in the heavens (Heb. 8:1), living in eternity to "make intercession for them" (Heb. 7:25). Here is Christ the Advocate, one who walked unscorched through mortal fires. The Advocate is literally the Father's Counselor, who from personal understanding petitions for mercy for mortals. The Petitioner asks not through mere pleading, but because he can boldly testify that he has paid the price of sin....God is playing celestial games if the Advocate is not a separate person from the Father, for the Romans-Hebrews verb for making intercession is an ancient legal term for appealing to another for aid. The same is true of the 1 Timothy-Hebrews noun "mediator." In both English and Greek the concept is "middleman," meaning a third person standing between two parties to bring them together. (Richard Lloyd Anderson, *Understanding Paul* [Salt Lake City, Utah: Deseret Book Co., 1983], pp. 99, 202, 216.)

In the ancient Christian church there was a group of faithful men who have come to be known as the Apostolic Fathers. Some of their writings have been collected and translated in an excellent book entitled *The Apostolic Fathers* (Nashville, Tennessee: Thomas Nelson Publishers, 1978, edited by Jack N. Sparks.) *The Apostolic Fathers* contains translations of the Epistle of Barnabas, the Didache, An Ancient Homily By An Unknown Author (traditionally referred to as 2 Clement), the Shepherd of Hermas, and the letters of Clement of Rome, Ignatius, and Polycarp.

Sparks has said the following about the importance of the Apostolic Fathers:

What Christian can help wondering what those people were like who received the gospel from the apostles?

What must it have been like to live in those days of raw beginnings, struggle, and dire persecution?...Wouldn't it be exciting to hear from those early leaders as they teach and interpret the Scriptures?

Impossible as it seems, given the turmoil and distress of the second century A.D., we do have some writings from them. As these Fathers preserved, copied, and passed on the Scriptures, they also wrote letters, instructions, and homilies....

Remember, too, that there is authority behind what these Fathers have to say—particularly Clement, bishop of Rome at the end of the first century; Ignatius, bishop of Antioch from the latter part of the first century through about a decade of the second; and Polycarp, bishop of Smyrna for about half of the second century. These leaders had direct connection with the apostles and others who knew the Lord in the flesh. They also held responsible and honored positions in early Christian communities. And need we add that they stood firmly under persecution, at least two of the four dying a martyr's death? Should we not therefore pay close attention to what they write? (*The Apostolic Fathers*, p. x.)

Like the New Testament, the writings of the Apostolic Fathers affirm the separateness of the Father and the Son and the subordination of the Savior to His Heavenly Father.

1 Clement:

The apostles received the gospel for us from Jesus Christ, and Jesus the Christ was sent from God. So Christ is from God, and the apostles are from Christ: thus both came in proper order by the will of God.

...God lives, and the Lord Jesus Christ lives, and the Holy Spirit,...

...the all-seeing God, Master of spirits and Lord of all flesh...chose the Lord Jesus Christ and us through him to be his own people....(*The Apostolic Fathers*, pp. 41, 49, 53.)

Ignatius:

...you may sing with one voice through Jesus Christ to the Father, so that he may both hear you and recognize you, through what you do well, as members of His Son.

Be eager, . . to be firmly set in the decrees of the Lord and the apostles so that "in whatsoever you do you may prosper"—in flesh and spirit, in faith and love, in the Son and the Father, at the beginning and at the end, together with your right reverend bishop and that worthily woven spiritual crown, your presbytery, and the godly deacons. Be subject to the bishop and to one another, as Jesus Christ in the flesh was subject to the Father and the apostles were subject to Christ and the Father,...

Do nothing apart from the bishop; keep your flesh as the temple of God; love unity; flee from divisions; be imitators of Jesus Christ as he is of his Father.

All of you are to follow the bishop as Jesus Christ follows the Father, and the presbytery as the apostles. (*The Apostolic Fathers*, pp. 78, 90, 106, 112.)

Polycarp:

Therefore gird up your loins and serve God in fear and truth; give up empty, vain discussion and the error of the crowd; believe in him who raised our Lord Jesus Christ from the dead and gave him glory and a throne at his right hand, to whom were subjected all things....

Now may the God and Father of our Lord Jesus Christ...give you a lot and portion with his saints, and to us along with you, and to all men who are under heaven who will believe in our Lord Jesus Christ and in his Father who raised him from the dead. (*The Apostolic Fathers*, pp. 127, 136. Notice that

Polycarp refers to the Father as "the God" of
Jesus Christ.)

Among the writings of the Apostolic Fathers is a book
that was greatly prized by the Early Church, the Shepherd
of Hermas. "The writing called the Shepherd of Hermas,"
says Albert C. Sundberg, "was highly regarded in the early church in both East and West. Irenaeus [bishop of Lyons
in the second century] cited it with approval; Clement of
Alexandria [a prominent early Christian writer] regarded
it as divinely spoken and by revelation...the Shepherd of
Hermas was not seriously questioned until the fourth century." ("The Making of the New Testament Canon," in
Charles Laymon, ed., *The Interpreter's One- Volume Commentary on the Bible* [Nashville, Tennessee: Abingdon Press,
1971], pp. 1221-1222; cf. Anderson, *Understanding Paul*, pp.
408-410; J. Reuben Clark, *Why the King James Version*, Classics
in Mormon Literature [Salt Lake City, Utah: Deseret Book
Co., reprint 1979], p. 237; Cyril C. Richardson, *Early Christian Fathers* [New York: Macmillan Publishing Co., Inc.,
1970], pp. 15-16.)

The Shepherd of Hermas:

> ...the Son of God does not appear in the
> guise of a slave, but appears with great power
> and authority....Because God planted the
> vineyard...and he turned it over to his Son.
> And the Son appointed the angels to protect
> every one of them [Christ's followers].
> ...a man cannot enter the Kingdom of God
> other than by the name of his Son, who was
> beloved by him....So no one can come to him
> [God] other than by his Son. (*The Apostolic
> Fathers*, pp. 215, 242.)

The Epistle of Barnabas was another highly regarded text
of the ancient Christian church. Such esteemed early Christian writers as Origen, Tertullian, and Clement of Alexan-

dria considered it to be scripture. (*The Ante-Nicene Fathers* [Grand Rapids, Michigan: William B. Eerdmans Publishing Co., reprint 1985], Vol. 2, pp. 354-355, 362, 366, 372, 459; Vol. 4, pp. 97, 424.) The epistle appears in one of the oldest New Testament manuscripts, the Codex Sinaiticus.

The Epistle of Barnabas:

> And furthermore, my brethren, consider this:...the Lord submitted to suffer for our souls—he who is Lord of the whole world, to whom God said at the foundation of the world: Let us make man in accord with our image and likeness.
>
> ...the Scripture is speaking about us when he [God] says to the Son: Let us make man in accord with our image and likeness, and let them rule over the beasts of the earth and the birds of heaven and the fish of the sea....These things he [God] said to the Son.
>
> ...the Father is making all things clear concerning his Son Jesus....David himself....prophesies: The Lord said to my Lord, "Sit at my right hand until I make your enemies a footstool for your feet." (*The Apostolic Fathers*, pp. 274, 278, 290.)

Yet another highly prized document of the Early Church was a book known as the Didache; its formal title was "The Teaching of the Lord to the Gentiles by the Twelve Apostles." The Didache, according to its translator, Robert A. Kraft, was a document "which was mentioned and highly regarded by many early Christian writers." (*The Apostolic Fathers*, p. 305.)

The Didache:

> We thank you, our Father, for the holy vine of David,..which you have made known to

us through Jesus your Servant. Glory to you
forever!

We thank you, our Father, for the life and
knowledge which you have made known to
us through Jesus your Servant. (*The Apostolic
Fathers*, p. 314.)

When one examines all of the Apostolic Fathers'
statements about the Godhead, it becomes apparent that
their use of "God" and "Lord" was very similar to Latter-
day Saint (LDS) usage. Judging from their writings, the
Apostolic Fathers felt free to apply the term "lord" to either
the Father or the Son. On occasion they would use the term
"God" to describe Christ, although they usually reserved
this title for the Father. They considered Christ to be the
savior-god of the Godhead. And, after all, Christ was and
is God the Son. So it comes as no surprise that there are
a few places in their writings where the Apostolic Fathers
apply the term "God" to Christ. Nevertheless, they
repeatedly expressed their belief that the Father and the
Son were two separate beings and that the Savior was
subordinate to His Heavenly Father.

Similarly, in Mormonism the term "Lord" is often used
to describe either the Father or the Son. The term or title
"God" is sometimes used to describe Christ. We know that
both the Father and the Son are Gods. Elohim is God the
Father. Jesus Christ is God the Son, Yahweh, the Son of
the Father. Therefore, we can use the term "God" for either
Heavenly Father or the Savior without confusing them as
the same person.

3

Jesus Is the Savior and Redeemer

Essential Doctrine:

According to the Bible, any church claiming to be the true church of Jesus Christ **must believe that Jesus Christ is the Savior and Redeemer of the world.**

Key Bible Passages:

Isa. 43:3 (3,11,25)	I am...thy God, the Holy One of Israel, thy Saviour.
Isa. 45:15	O God of Israel, the Saviour.
Matt. 1:21	Jesus shall save his people from their sins.
Luke 1:47	My spirit hath rejoiced in God my saviour.
John 3:16-17 (16-20)	God so loved the world that he gave his only begotten Son, that the world through him might be saved.
Acts 2:21 (16-21)	Whosoever shall call on the...Lord shall be saved.
Acts 13:23	He raised unto Israel a Saviour, Jesus.
Rom. 6:6 (3-7)	Our old man is crucified with him, that the body of sin might be destroyed.

2 Cor. 5:21	He hath made him to be sin for us, who knew no sin (Christ); that we might be made the righteousness of God in him.
Eph. 5:2	Christ hath loved us, and given himself for us an offering and a sacrifice to God.
Philip. 3:20 (20-21)	We look for the Saviour, the Lord Jesus Christ.
1 Tim. 4:10	We trust in the living God, who is the Saviour of all men.
Heb. 5:8-9	Though he were a Son, being made perfect, he became the author of eternal salvation.
Heb. 10:12 (10-12)	This man (Christ), after he had offered one sacrifice for sins for ever, sat down on the right hand of God.
1 Jn. 2:2 (1-2)	He is the propitiation for our sins, and for the sins of the whole world.
1 Jn. 4:14	The Father sent the Son to be the Saviour of the world.

References for Further Study:

1. See sections 1, 2, 4, 5, 6 and 8 of this book.

4

Jesus Christ Is Jehovah

Essential Doctrine:

According to the Bible, any church claiming to be the true church of Jesus Christ **must believe that Jesus Christ is Jehovah (Yahweh) come to earth and that Elohim (or El, for short) was Yahweh-Christ's father**.

Key Bible Passages:

This doctrine is clearly esablished by comparing Old Testament passages which refer to Jehovah with New Testament passages which refer to Jesus Christ, showing that they identify the same characteristics and the same individual.

Note: The term LORD, written in all-capital letters in the Bible, represents the term Yahweh, or Jehovah.

Gen. 17:1	Jehovah told Abraham: I am the Almighty god. (Gen. 35:11)
Rev. 1:8	Christ told John: I am...the Almighty.
Ex. 3:14 (14-16)	Jehovah told Moses, Say unto the children of Israel, I AM hath sent me unto you.
Jn. 8:58 (55-59)	Jesus said, Before Abraham was, I am.

27

Deut. 1:32-33   Jehovah accompanied Israel in their exodus from Egypt.

1 Cor. 10:1-4   Christ accompanied Israel in their exodus from Egypt.

Ps. 96:13   Jehovah comes to judge the earth.

Jn. 5:22-23   The Father judgeth no man, but hath committed all judgment unto the Son.

Is. 43:3, 11   Jehovah is the Saviour. (Is. 49:26, 60:16)

Luke 2:11   Unto you is born...a Savior, which is Christ the Lord.

Isa. 48:17   Jehovah is the Redeemer. (Isa. 49:7)

Rom. 3:24   Redemption is in Christ Jesus.

Isa. 44:6   Jehovah is the first and the last.

Rev. 1:17   Christ is the first and the last.

Isa. 45:11-12   Jehovah made the earth and created man. (Isa. 37:16)

Jn. 1:3   All things were made by Christ. (Col.
(1-3)   1:16)

Isa. 45:23   Every knee shall bow and every tongue shall swear to Jehovah.

Rom. 14:10-11   Every knee shall bow and every tongue shall confess to Christ.

Hos. 13:4   There is no Savior besides Jehovah.

Acts. 4:12   Christ is the only name given whereby
(10-12)   we must be saved.

Zech. 12:10   They shall look upon Jehovah whom they have pierced.

Jn. 19:34 (34-37)   The soldiers pierced Christ's side.

| Zech. 14:5 | Jehovah shall come, with all the saints. |
| 1 Thes. 3:13 | Christ shall come, with all the saints. |

| Zech. 14:9 | Jehovah shall be king over all the earth. |
| Rev. 11:15 | The kingdoms of this world are become the kingdoms of our Lord; Christ shall reign for ever and ever. |

References for Further Study:

1. Otto Eissfeldt, "El and Yahweh," *Journal of Semitic Studies*, Vol. 1, 1956, pp. 25-30.

2. Eugene Seaich, *Ancient Texts and Mormonism* (Sandy, Utah: Mormon Miscellaneous, 1983), pp. 2-22.

3. *Mormonism, The Dead Sea Scrolls, and the Nab Hammadi Texts* (Murray, Utah: Sounds of Zion, 1980), pp. 21-26.

4. Paul Hoskisson, "Another Significance of the Golden Calf Motif," in John Welch, ed., *Tinkling Cymbals* (Provo, Utah: Unpublished manuscript, 1978), pp. 55-70, available from the Foundation for Ancient Research and Mormon Studies (FARMS, for short), P. O. Box 7113, University Station, Provo, Utah 84602.

5. See sections 1, 2, 3, 5, 6 and 8 of this book.

Explanatory Notes:

There is much confusion on this point because of the erroneous belief that El and Yahweh were the same deity. This belief is held by the Jehovah's Witnesses and by most of the fundamentalist churches. However, there is a tremendous amount of evidence for the fact that anciently El and Yahweh were originally considered to be two seperate deities, El being the father-god and Yahweh the son-god.

Comparisons of the Old and New Testaments make it clear that Christ was Yahweh come to earth, and yet Christ said He had a Heavenly Father over Him. Christ prayed to His Heavenly Father. Christ said His Father was greater than He was. The Savior sits on the right hand of His

Heavenly Father. We even read of "the God" of Jesus Christ. (Ephesians 1:3, 17; 2 Corinthians 11:31; John 20:17; Matthew 27:46; Revelation 3:11-12.), etc. If Christ was Yahweh, then who was Yahweh-Christ's father? The answer is obvious: Elohim (or El, for short), the father-god of the ancient Hebrew pantheon.

As an aside note, mention should be made of the evidence for the Mormon emendation of Psalms 110:1. Although the Hebrew of the verse now represents Yahweh as speaking to the "Lord," Mormons assert that this verse has been tampered with and that it should represent Elohim speaking to Yahweh, because it is clear that the Father is speaking to the Son. Interestingly, some early Christian texts assert that in this verse God the Father is speaking to His Son, Jesus Christ. (*The Apostolic Fathers,* pp. 38, 290; cf. Mathew 22:44; Mark 12:36; Luke 20:42.)

5

Jesus Is the Creator of the World

Essential Doctrine:

According to the Bible, any church claiming to be the true church of Jesus Christ **must believe that Jesus created this world, doing so in fulfillment of his Heavenly Father's will**.

Key Bible Passages:

Christ Is the Creator

2 Kgs. 19:15	O Lord God of Israel...thou hast made heaven and earth.
Job 10:8 (8-12)	Thine hands have made me and fashioned me together.
Ps. 33:6	By the word of the Lord were the heavens made, and all the host of them.
Isa. 41:20	The hand of the Lord hath done this, and the Holy One of Israel hath created it.
Isa. 42:5	God the Lord, he that created the heavens and spread forth the earth.
Isa. 44:24	Thus saith the LORD, thy Redeemer, I am the LORD that maketh all things.

Isa. 45:12 (12-15)	I have made the earth, and created man upon it.
Isa. 65:17	Behold, I create new heavens and a new earth.
Jer. 51:15 (15-16)	Christ hath made the earth and heaven by his power.
John 1:3 (1-4)	All things were made by him.
Acts 7:50	Christ's hand made all these things.
Col. 1:16 (14-17)	All things were created by him, and for him.
Heb. 1:10	Thou, Lord...hast laid the foundation of the earth, and the heavens are the works of thy hands.
Heb. 11:3	The worlds were framed by the word of God.
Rev. 4:11	Christ hast created all things, and for thy pleasure they are and were created.

Christ Created the Earth Under Direction of God the Father

Gen. 1:26 (26-27)	God said, let us make man in our image, after our likeness. (See 1:27; 3:22)
Rom. 8:29	For whom he did foreknow, he also did predestinate to be conformed to the image of his Son, that he might be the firstborn among many brethren.
Eph. 3:9	God, who created all things by Jesus Christ.
Heb. 1:1-2 (1-3)	God...hath spoken by his Son, whom he hath appointed heir of all things, by whom also he made the worlds.

References for Further Study:

1. Keith Norman, "Ex Nihilo: The Development of the Doctrines of God and Creation in Early Christianity." *BYU Studies* (Spring, 1977), pp. 291-318.

2. Robert Wilken, *The Christians as the Romans Saw Them* (London: Yale University Press, 1984), pp. 88-89.
3. See sections 1, 2, 3, 4, 6 and 8 of this book.

Explanatory Notes:

The earth was created out of already existing matter. This is an important point which has significant implications for a correct understanding of the nature of God.

The idea that the world was created out of nothing, or "ex nihilo," is emphatically proclaimed by Catholicism and Protestantism, but it was *not* a doctrine of the early Christian church.

The Bible does not teach that the world was created "ex nihilo"; rather, it teaches just the opposite. I quote Keith Norman:

...Joseph Smith took issue with the standard translation and interpretation of the opening verse in the Bible: "In the beginning God created the heaven and the earth." Although the Hebrew word "bara," here translated "created," is usually reserved in the Old Testament for God's activity in forming the world and all things in it, synonymous terms and phrases scattered throughout the Hebrew scriptures take the force out of any attempt to use this fact as evidence that an "ex nihilo" creation is being described in Genesis 1. The most common of these synonyms are "yasar," to shape or form, and "asah," to make or produce. In a study of the Hebrew conception of the created order, Luis Stadelmann insists that both "bara" and "yasar" carry the anthropomorphic sense of fashioning, while "asah" connotes a more general idea of production. Throughout the Old Testament the image is that of the craftsman shaping the vessel out of clay, or the waver at his loom. The heavens and the earth are "the work of God's hand." Thus, Joseph Smith, who had studied Hebrew, preferred to translate the verb "bara" as "to organize"....

Frank M. Cross concludes that it was the creation "ex nihilo" tradition which prompted the translation of Genesis

1:1 found in the King James and similar versions. According the *The Interpreter's Bible*, the Hebrew "bere sit" [of
Gen. 1:1] would be more properly rendered "In the beginning of" rather than simply "In the beginning." Thus the
first verse of Genesis does not stand apart from the following narative as a kind of summarizing prelude, but merges
naturally with verse two, and we might correctly translate,
as E.A. Speiser suggests, "When God set about to create
heaven and earth, the world being then a formless waste...."
    The King James translation of Genesis 1:2, which renders
the Hebrew as "void," has...lent support to the creation "ex
nihilo" theory, whereas actually the word always occurs in
the Old Testament in tandem with "tohy" ("formless"),
describing a "formless waste"....
    In fact the Old Testament account of the creation, from
Genesis 1 and consistently throughout, supports the radical
departure of Joseph Smith from the orthodox "ex nihilo"
dogma....
    The Septuagint, when referring to God as the Creator,
avoided forms of the word "demiourgos" in favor of the
verb "ktidzo" and its derivatives. Homer...had used "ktidzo" in the sense of "to build" or "establish" a city, and the
word still carried its architectural connotation into New
Testament times.... For the most part the New Testament
was composed in Greek, and its terminology was greatly
influenced by the Septuagint. Thus the term "demiourgous"
is used only once, in Hebrews 11:10, which has no direct
reference to the creation. The most common verb to
describe the creative activity is "ktidzo" but it is followed
in frequency by "poieo" (to make or produce, especially of
art), and "plasso" (to form, mold, shape or fashion), both
of which are used synonymously. ("Ex Nihilo: The development of the doctrines of God and Creation in Early Christianity," pp. 295-301.)

6

Jesus the Firstborn

Essential Doctrine:

According to the Bible, any church claiming to be the true church of Jesus Christ **must believe that Jesus Christ was the firstborn of our Heavenly Father's spirit children in a premortal spirit existence prior to mortal life on this earth.**

Key Bible Passages:

Jesus Christ Is the Son of God the Father

Matt. 3:17 (16-17)	This is my beloved Son, in whom I am well pleased.
Matt. 16:16 (13-17)	Thou art the Christ, the Son of the living God.
Matt. 17:5 (4-9)	This is my beloved Son, in whom I am well pleased.
Matt. 27:43	For he said, I am the Son of God.
Luke 1:32 (31-35)	He shall...be called the Son of the Highest.
John 1:14 (1,14)	We beheld his glory, the glory as of the only begotten of the Father, full of grace and truth.
John 1:18	The only begotten Son, which is in the bosom of the Father.
John 3:16 (16-18)	God so loved the world, that he gave his only begotten Son.

John 3:35	The Father loveth the Son, and hath given all things into his hand.
John 5:26 (17-31)	The Father hath given to the Son to have life in himself.
John 10:36	Christ said, I am the Son of God.
John 16:15 (15-16)	All things that the Father hath are mine.
John 17:1 (1-2)	Father...glorify thy Son, that thy Son also may glorify thee.
John 20:21	As my Father hath sent me, even so send I you.
Acts. 13:33	As it is written in the second psalm, Thou art my Son, this day have I begotten thee.
Rom. 15:6	Glorify God, even the Father of our Lord Jesus Christ.
Col. 1:13 (12-19)	The Father hath translated us into the kingdom of his dear Son.
Heb. 1:2 (1-4)	God hath spoken by his Son, whom he hath appointed heir of all things.
Heb. 1:5 (5-8)	Unto which of the angels hath God said at any time, Thou art my Son, this day have I begotten thee?
Heb. 7:28	The oath...maketh the Son, who is consecrated for evermore.

Jesus Christ Is the Firstborn Son of God the Father

Ps. 89:27 (27-37)	I will make him my firstborn, higher than the kings of the earth.
Isa. 41:4	I the Lord, the first, and with the last; I am he.
John 1:1 (1-5)	In the beginning was the Word, and the Word was with God, and the Word was God.
Rom. 8:29 (29-30)	Of his Son, that he might be the firstborn among many brethren.
Col. 1:15 (13-15)	Christ is the firstborn of every creature.

Heb. 1:6	He bringeth in the firstbegotten into the
(1-6)	world, he saith, And let all the angels of God worship him.
Heb. 12:23	To the general assembly and church of
(22-24)	the firstborn.
Rev. 1:11	I am Alpha and Omega, the first and the
(8-18)	last.
Rev. 3:14	The Amen...the beginning of the creation of God.

References for Further Study:

1. Benjamin Urrutia and Raphael Patai, *American Anthropologist*, Vol. 74. 1972, pp. 1598-1599, and Urrutia in *Ibid*, Vol 75, 1973, pp. 1180-1181.
2. See also sections 1, 2, 3, 4, 5 and 8 of this book.

Explanatory Notes:

The verses cited from Colossians and Revelation presuppose the doctrine of pre-mortal existence. These verses are telling us that Christ was the "firstborn" of "every creature" in the premortal existence and that the Savior was "the beginning" of God's spiritual "creation" before the foundation of the world (cf. John 17:5, 24; Hebrews 1:6).

Colossians 1:15 could not possibly refer to Christ's physical birth since obviously millions of animals and millions of our Heavenly Father's children were born before the Savior was born into this world. Paul is here speaking of Christ's spiritual birth in the pre-mortal existence.

Some assert that "firstborn" as it is applied to Christ in Colossians 1:15 simply refers to His preeminence and that it is not to be taken as literally saying that Christ was the "first one born" of every creature.

In Colossians 1:18 Christ is referred to as "the firstborn from the dead; that in all things he might have the preeminence." Christ's preeminence over all those of the resurrection is certainly pointed out. But it should be observed that the term "firstborn" here also applies to Christ' numerical order in the resurrection, since He was the first one whom the Father resurrected. (Cf. 1 Corinthians 15:20.)

If in Colossians 1:18 "firstborn" refers to both preeminence and numerical order, then it is logical to assume that it has the same dual application in Colossians 1:15. Therefore, I would argue that the term "firstborn" as it is applied to Christ in Colossians 1:15 refers to His preeminence *and* to His being the firstborn of our Heavenly Father's spirit children in the preexistence.

This interpretation is strengthened by Revelation 3:14, and by Hebrews 1:6, which refers to Christ as "the firstbegotten." The Greek word for "firstbegotten" is "prototokos," which means "the first one begotten" or "the first one born." This term could not possibly apply to Christ's mortal birth, but it applies perfectly to His premortal birth as the firstbegotten of Heavenly Father's spirit children in the premortal life.

Revelation 3:14 has posed a special problem for some Catholic and Protestant commentators because it states that Christ was "the beginning" of God's creation, which contradicts their belief that the Father and the Son are the same person and that Christ is "uncreated." Fundamentalist scholars have attempted to read "the ruler of" as opposed to "the beginning of" in this verse. Such a reading seems forced. The Greek word in question in this passage is "arche," which normally means "beginning" or "commencement." This is exactly how "arche" is used in Phillipians 4:15; Colossians 1:18; 2 Thessalonians 2:13; Hebrews 1:10; 3:14; 7:3; 2 Peter 3:4; Acts 11:15; 1 John 1:1; 2:7, 13-14, 24; 3:8, 11; 2 John 5-6; and in other places.

The apostle Paul was the author of Hebrews and Colossians. Paul was also a very learned Jew before he joined the church. He was intimately acquainted with Judaism. He quoted from the Hebrew Old Testament on many occasions. And he wrote the epistle of Hebrews to a group of Jewish Christians. (Leon Morris, "Hebrews," in F.

Gaebelein, ed., *The Expositor's Bible Commentary*, Vol. 12 [Grand Rapids, Michigan: Zondervan Publishing House, 1981], pp. 45.) Therefore, let us examine the meaning of the word "firsborn" in the Old Testament.

In the Old Testament the word "firstborn" almost always applies to numerical order, as well as to preeminence, among males, i.e. the first son of the family. In ancient Hebrew culture the firstborn son had the right to twothirds of the inheritance and to preferential treatment. (Barry Beitzel, "The Right of the Firstborn in the Old Testament," in W. C. Kaser and R. F. Youngblood, eds., *A Tribute to Gleason Archer: Essays on the Old Testament* [Chicago, Illinois: Moody Press, 1986], pp. 179190.) He was preeminent among the family's children. There are a few instances in Old Testament history when a younger son replaced the oldest son as the firstborn of the family. Nevertheless, even in those rare cases it was still clearly understood who the natural firstborn was.

There are a few places in the Old Testament where the term "firstborn" is used metaphorically, such as Exodus 4:22 and Jeremiah 31:9. The metaphorical usage in these two verses is effective precisely because of the normal, literal meaning of the word "firstborn." In both verses the authors understood what "firstborn" really meant. In the very next verse after Exodus 4:22, the Lord threatens to kill all of the Egyptians' firstborn children if the Israelites are not released. In Jeremiah 31:9 the Lord says, "I am a father to Israel, and Ephraim is my firstborn," again clearly displaying an understanding of the actual meaning of the word "firstborn."

The Hebrew word for "firstborn" is "bekore," which means "the first one born," "the first male born," or "eldest son." (Reuben Alcalay, *The Complete Hebrew-English Dictionary* [Jerusalem, Israel: Massada Publishing Co., 1981], p. 239.) The Hebrew root from which "bekore" is derived is "bakar," meaning "to burst the womb," "to bear or make early fruit" (of woman or tree), or "to bring forth first child."

In summary, in the Old Testament "firstborn" means "the first one born" or "the first male born" (except in those rare instances when it is used metaphorically or when a younger son assumed the oldest son's role as the family's firstborn), while at the same time it refers to preeminence, the preeminence of the firstborn. (Cf. *The New Smith's Bible Dictionary* [New York: Doubleday, 1966], pp. 109110.)

Interestingly, in 2 Clement, in an allegorical interpretation of Genesis 1:27, Christ is spoken of as a creation of God. (*The Apostolic Fathers*, pp. 66-67.)

The Mormon doctrine of Christ as the firstborn of our Heavenly Father's spirit children is best understood in conjunction with the LDS belief in a heavenly mother. I quote Milton R. Hunter for a brief summary of this belief:

When light burst forth from heaven in revelations to the Prophet Joseph Smith, a more complete understanding of man—especially regarding his personal relationship to Deity—was received than could be found in all of the holy scriptures combined. The...existence of a Heavenly Mother, as well as a Heavenly Father, became established facts in Mormon theology. A complete realization that we are the offspring of Heavenly Parents—that we were begotten and born into the spirit world and grew to maturity in that realm—became an integral part of Mormon philosophy....

Jesus is man's spiritual brother. We dwelt with Him in the spirit world as members of that large society of eternal intelligences, which included our Heavenly Parents and all the personages who have become mortal beings upon this earth or who ever shall come here to dwell. In that spirit-creation, when we became children of God, Jesus was the "firstborn," and so He is our eldest brother. (*The Gospel Through the Ages* [Salt Lake City, Utah: Deseret Book Co., 1958], pp. 98-99, 21.

Seaich has compiled evidence that a belief in a Heavenly Mother was also found among the ancient Hebrews and the early Christians. [*Mormonism, The Dead Sea Scrolls, and the Nag Hammadi Texts*, pp. 2632; *Ancient Texts and Mormonism*, pp. 2325.])

On a related note, it should be pointed out that Satan was also one of our Heavenly Father's spirit children and was at one time a member of the Divine Council, but he and those who followed him were cast down from heaven. (Barker, *Apostasy from the Divine Church*, pp. 44-45; R.S. Kluger, *Satan in the Old Testament* (Northwestern University Press, 1967); Robert F. Smith, "Satan: Notes on the Gods" (Unpublished paper, 1986, copy in the author's possession); E. Theodore Mullen, *The Assembly of the Gods: The Divine Council in Canaanite and Early Hebrew Literature*, Harvard Semitic Monograph Series, No. 24 (Chicago, Illinois: Scholars Press, 1980), pp. 274-278; cf. Bo Reicke, "The Epistles of James, Peter, and Jude," *The Anchor Bible* (Garden City, New York: Doubleday and Company, Inc., 1964), p. 167; Seaich, *Ancient Texts and Mormonism*, pp. 36-42; James Efird, "Satan," in Paul J. Achtemeier, ed., *Harper's Bible Dictionary* (San Francisco, California: Harper & Row, Publishers, 1985), pp. 908-909.) This, of course, means that Christ and Satan were brothers in the pre-mortal existence, although even then the Savior was superior to Satan.

7

Man's Pre-mortal Existence

Essential Doctrine:

According to the Bible and other ancient Christian sources, any church claiming to be the true church of Jesus Christ **must believe that all mankind lived wih our Heavenly Father as His spirit sons and daughters in a premortal state before coming to this earth.**

Key Bible Passages:

All Mankind Are Spirit Children of Heavenly Father

Num. 16:22	O God, the God of the spirits of all flesh,...
Job 32:8	But there is a spirit in man: and the inspiration of the Almighty giveth them understanding.
Job 33:4	The Spirit of God hath made me, and the breath of the Almighty hath given me life.
Ps. 82:6	Ye are gods; and all of you are children of the most High.
Eccl. 12:7	The spirit shall return unto God who gave it.
Isa. 42:5	He that giveth breath...and spirit to them that walk.
Hosea 1:10	Said unto them, ye are the sons of the living God.

Luke 23:46	Father, into thy hands I commend my spirit: and having said thus, he gave up the ghost.
Acts 7:59	Stephen, calling upon God, saying, Lord Jesus, receive my spirit.
Acts 17:29 (28-29)	We are the offspring of God.
Rom. 8:16 (16-17)	The Spirit beareth witness with our spirit, that we are the children of God.
Heb. 12:9	We have had fathers of our flesh who corrected us, shall we not be in subjection unto the Father of spirits?

Man's Premortal Existence

Num. 27:16	The Lord, the God of the spirits of all flesh.
Job 38:7 (1-7)	When I laid the foundations of the earth,...when the morning stars sang together, and all the sons of God shouted for joy.
Isa. 14:13-14 (12-15)	Lucifer said, I will exalt my throne above the stars of God; I will be like the most High.
Jer. 1:5 (4-5)	Before I formed thee in the belly I knew thee;... and I ordained thee a prophet unto the nations.
Zech. 12:1	The Lord, which...formeth the spirit of man within him.
Luke 10:18 (17-20)	I beheld Satan as lightning fall from heaven.
John 1:2 (1-2,14)	The same was in the beginning with God.
John 8:58 (58-59)	I say uno you, before Abraham was, I am.
John 9:2 (1-2)	Master, who did sin, this man, or his parents, that he was born blind?
John 16:28 (27-30)	I came forth from the Father, and am come into the world.

John 17:5 (3-5,24)	O Father, glorify thou me with the glory which I had with thee before the world was.
Rom. 8:29 (28-30)	For whom he did foreknow, he also did predestinate to be conformed to the image of his Son, that he might be the firstborn among many brethren.
Eph. 1:4 (3-6)	He hath chosen us in him before the foundation of the world.
Jude 1:6 (5-6)	The angels which kept not their first estate, but left their own habitation, he hath reserved unto judgment.
Rev. 12:7 (7-8)	There was war in heaven: Michael and his angels fought against the dragon. The Devil and his angels were cast out into the earth.

References for Further Study:

1. Eugene Seaich, *Mormonism, The Dead Sea Scrolls, and the Nag Hammadi Texts*, (Murray, Utah: Sounds of Zion, 1980), pp. 4-17.

2. R. G. Hamerton-Kelly, *Pre-Existence, Wisdom, and the Son of Man*, (Cambridge, 1973).

3. Joseph Fielding McConkie, "Premortal Existence, Foreordinations, and Heavenly Councils." in C. Wilfred Griggs, ed., *Apocryphal Writings and the Latter-day Saints* (Provo, Utah: Brigham Young University, Religious Studies Center, 1986), pp. 173-198.

4. James L. Barker, *Apostasy From the Divine Church* (Salt Lake City, Utah: Bookcraft Publishing Co., reprint 1984), pp. 44-49.

5. Hugh Nibley, "Treasures in the Heavens," in Truman Madsen, ed., *Nibley on the Timely and the Timeless* (Provo, Utah: Brigham Young University, Religious Studies Center, 1978), pp. 49-84.

6. See sections 5 and 6 of this book.

Explanatory Notes:

I quote Seaich for a partial summary of the evidence for pre-mortal existence:

> [The] "heavenly council" was an early form of the pre-existent Community [of mankind], of which the sectaries at Qumran [i.e. the people of the Dead Sea Scrolls] claimed to be a living part (4 Q Serek Shirah, the "Angelic Liturgy"). The pre-existent Community of apocalyptic became the pre-existent Church of Primitive Christianity (Albert Schweizer, *The Mysticism of the Apostle Paul*, reprint N.Y., 1968, 102ff, 116; Jean Danielou, *The Theology of Jewish Christianity*, London, 1964, 4, 262-301),...
>
> But the pre-existence of individual souls is even more widely attested in early Jewish and Christian literature. We have already referred to the Essene and Philonic doctrines of pre-existent souls. The Wisdom of Solomon speaks of these individual souls as follows: "As a child I was by nature well endowed, and a good soul fell to my lot; or rather, being good, I entered an undefiled body" (8:19-20). Apocalyptists generally taught that these souls dwelled in a special chamber (or chambers), awaiting their turn to descend into bodies (4 Ezra 4:37-43; 2 Baruch 23:3-5; 2 Enoch 23:4-5; 49:2).
>
> The rabbis for a time held the same belief. In the Talmud and Midrash, for example, the special chamber is called the "guf" (Abodah Zarah 5a; Yebamoth 62:1; Sifre 143b), or "araboth" (Chagiga 12b). According to the Genesis Rabbah, God took counsel with the pre-existent souls before creating the earth (8).

The Tenhuma Pekude actually records a conversation in which God explains to one of these souls how it is to descend into matter, and that if it will obey the Torah righteously, it will one day return to his presence to enjoy everlasting bliss (3). (See also F. Weber, *Judishce Theologie*, Leipzig, 1897, 212, 225ff., for a treatment of Jewish pre-existence doctrine.)

The Church Fathers continued to teach human pre-existence for several centuries, as attested in the works of Origen, Justin Martyr, Cyril of Jerusalem, Pierius, John of Jerusalem, Refinus, Nemesius, and many others. (Hastings, *Encyclopedia of Religion and Ethics* x:239). "Orthodox" Christianity is therefore beginning to grudgingly admit that pre-existence was an important part of the Church's original teaching....

Recent scholars have begun to discover a growing number of passages in the New Testament which are dependent upon the doctrine of pre-existence. The disciples' question concerning the blind man ("Master, who did sin, this man, or his parents, that he was born blind?" John 9:2) shows that they recognized the possibility of having sinned in a pre-existent life (*Interpreter's Dictionary of the Bible* III:869). [And Christ accepted the apostles' premise and simply answered that neither the man nor his parents had sinned.]

Hamerton-Kelly [in his book, *Pre-existence, Wisdom, and the Son of Man*] has exhaustively examined many other New Testament passages which presuppose the doctrine of pre-existence." (*Mormonism, the Dead Sea Scrolls, and the Nag Hammadi Texts*, pp. 6-8.)

Hugh Nibley, an authority on early Christian history, has accurately summed up the situation: "We know today,...

that the early Christians believed firmly in the pre-existence." (Nibley, "The Early Christian Church in Light of Some Newly Discovered Papyri from Egypt" [Provo, Utah: Brigham Young University Extension Publications, 1964], p. 17; cf. Anderson, *Understanding Paul*, pp. 274-277, 307, 346-350.)

8

Man Has the Potential to Attain Godhood

Essential Doctrine:

According to the Bible and other ancient Christian sources, any church claiming to be the true church of Jesus Christ **must believe that men and women have the potential to attain Godhood, to be deified**.

Key Bible Passages:

Ps. 82:6 (1-8)	Ye are Gods...all of you are children of the most high.
Matt. 5:48	Be ye therefore perfect, even as your Father which is in heaven is perfect.
John 10:34 (34-36)	Is it not written in your law, I said, ye are Gods?
Acts 17:29 (24-29)	We are the offspring of God.
Rom. 8:16-17 (14-21)	We are the children of God, and if children, then heirs of God, and joint-heirs with Christ. We may be glorified together.
1 Cor. 2:9	Eye hath not seen the things which God has prepared for them that love him.
2 Cor. 3:18	We beheld the glory of the Lord, and are changed into the same image from glory to glory.

Gal. 4:7 (1-7)	Thou art a son, and if a son, then an heir of God through Christ.
Eph. 4:11-13	He gave some prophets and apostles, for the perfecting of the saints, till we all come...unto a perfect man.
2 Peter 1:4	There are given to us great and precious promises, that by these ye might be partakers of the divine nature.
1 Jn. 3:2 (1-3)	We are the sons of God, when Christ shall appear, we shall be like him.
Rev. 3:21	Him that overcometh will...sit...in my throne.

References for Further Study:

1. Keith Norman, "Divinization: the Forgotten Teaching of Early Christianity," *Sunstone* (Winter 1975), pp. 15-19.

2. Phillip Barlow, "Unorthodox Orthodoxy: The Idea of Deification in Christian History," *Sunstone* (September/October 1983), pp. 13-18.

3. Rodney Turner, "The Doctrine of Godhood in the New Testament," *Principles of the Gospel in Practice,* , 1985 (Sperry Symposium (Salt Lake City: Randall Book Co.), pp. 21-38.

Explanatory Notes:

Not only does the doctrine of man's ability to attain Godhood appear in several places in the New Testament, but this teaching—known as theosis, deification, or divinization—can also be found in the writings of numerous early Christian theologians including Origen, Irenaeus, Clement of Alexandria, Basil of Caesaria, Appollinaris of Laodicea, and Hippolytus.

The author of Hebrews states that God "hath appointed" Christ heir "of all things." (1:1-2; cf. 1 Peter 3:22) In Romans 8:15-17 we learn that the faithful are "joint-heirs with Christ." Therefore, if we are faithful we will inherit all that Christ has received from our Heavenly Father, i.e. Godhood. In

Revelations 3:21 we read this: "To him that overcometh will I [Christ] grant to sit with me in my throne, *Even as I also overcame, and am set down with my Father in His throne.*"

Hippolytus, the bishop of Portus at the beginning of the third century, had this to say about man's potential:

> And thou shalt be a companion of the Deity, and a co-heir with Christ, no longer enslaved with lusts or passions, and never again wasted by disease, for thou hast become God....(*Refutations of Heresies* 10:30.)

Elsewhere Hippolytus taught that we "may dwell in expectation of receiving what the Father has granted to the Son." (See Elaine Pagels, *The Gnostic Gospels* [New York: Vintage Books, 1979], p. 107. It should be noted that Pagels discusses both Gnostic *and* early Christian beliefs.)

Methodius, bishop of Olympus and Patara at the end of the third century, stated that Christ "was made man that we might be made God." (See S. Angus, *The Mystery Religions; A Study in the Religious Background of Early Christianity* [New York: Dover Publications, Inc.], pp. 105-107.)

There is also considerable information available from ancient sources which shows that the early Christians believed in a Divine Council of deities, of which the Godhead is a part, and over which the Godhead presides. See the following references for further information:

1. Eugene Seaich, *Ancient Texts and Mormonism*, (Sandy, Utah: Mormon Miscellaneous, 1983), pp. 2-23.

2. Eugene Seaich, *Mormonism, The Dead Sea Scrolls, and The Nag Hammadi Texts*, (Murray, Utah: Sounds of Zion, 1980), pp. 21-26.

3. Joseph Fielding McConkie, "Premortal Existence, Foreordinations, and Heavenly Councils," in C. Griggs, ed., *Apocraphal Writings and the Latter-day Saints* (Provo, Utah, 1986), pp. 173-198.

4. E. Theodore Mullen, *The Assembly of the Gods: The Divine Council in Canaanite and Early Hebrew Literature* (Chicago: Scholars Press, 1980).

5. William F. Albright, *Yahweh and the Gods of Canaan* (London: School of Oriental and African Studies, 1968), pp. 191-193.

6. Julian Morgenstern, "The Divine Triad in Biblical Mythology," *Journal of Biblical Literature* (JBL), 64, 1945, pp. 15-37.

7. H. Wheeler Robinson, "The Council of Yahweh," JBL, 45, 1944, pp. 151-157.

8. Kluger, *Satan in the Old Testament* (Northwestern University Press, 1967).

9. See also sections 1, 2, 3, 4, 5, 6, and 7 of this book.

9

Prophets Function as Spokesmen for God

Essential Doctrine:

According to the Bible, any church claiming to be the true church of Jesus Christ **must have prophets who convey knowledge and instructions from God to the church members and to the world.**

Key Bible Passages:

Gen. 20:7 (1-7)	For he is a prophet, and he shall pray for thee, and thou shalt live.
Num. 11:29	Would God that all the Lord's people were prophets.
Deut. 18:15	The Lord will raise up unto thee a Prophet.
Judg. 6:8	The Lord sent a prophet unto the children of Israel.
Amos 3:7	Surely the Lord God will do nothing but he revealeth his secret unto his servants the prophets.
Mt. 10:40-41	He that receiveth a prophet in the name of a prophet, shall receive a prophet's reward.
Mt. 23:34	I send unto you prophets, and wise men.

Acts 3:22-23	A prophet shall the Lord your God raise up unto you,...and every soul who shall not hear that prophet shall be destroyed.
Eph. 2:20 (19-21)	The church is built upon the foundation of the apostles and prophets.
Eph. 4:11-14	And he gave prophets...for the perfecting of the saints, for the work of the ministry, for the edifying of the body of Christ.

References for Further Study:

1. See sections for this book.

Explanatory Notes:

Prophets function as spokesmen for God. They have the responsibility to convey God's will to the people, bringing them knowledge and instructions to guide their growth and progress and to warn them of impending harm and evil. They speak to man in behalf of all members of the Godhead and the Divine Council. E. Theodore Mullen states the following:

> The prophetic material makes it clear that the prophet was viewed as the messenger of Yahweh....As G. E. Wright has asserted, when the prophet proclaimed Yahweh's indictment of Israel, as in Isaiah 1:2 or Micah 6:2, the background must be seen as that of the divine council. In like manner, F. M. Cross has noted that the address of the divine assembly is marked by plural imperatives, as well as by the usage of the first person plural form of address (cf. Genesis 1:26; 3:22; 11:7; Judges 5:3, 23; Isaiah 35:3-4 40:1-8; 48:20-21; 51:7-10; 57:14; 62:10-12; Zechariah 3:4)....

That the divine council formed the background for prophecy was first shown beyond dispute by H. W. Robinson. This position was further established by F. M. Cross....

This is the true prophet's claim to authority. From the pronouncement of the council he receives the decree that he is to deliver. Those prophets who have not participated in the council are unable to proclaim the divine decree." (*The Assembly of the Gods*, pp. 215-221.)

Joseph Fielding McConkie has also furnished us with valuable information about the role of prophets as spokesmen for the Divine Council, especially with regard to Jeremiah 23:

The root from which "counsel" or "secret" comes [in Jeremiah 23:18, 21-22] is the Hebrew "sod" (also rendered "sodh," or "sode"), which should have been translated "council," which is the way it reads, for instance, in the New English and Jerusalem Bibles....After persuing the etymology of "sod," Raymond Brown concludes that its basic meaning is "council or assembly." He further concludes that in our Jeremiah text we are clearly dealing with a heavenly assembly.

What Jeremiah is telling us, then, is that all true prophets will profess to have stood in a heavenly council or assembly, where they received their message and the commission to declare it. Any not so professing are, according to Jeremiah's standard, to be rejected as false prophets....

H. Wheeler Robinson, in his article on "the Council of Yahweh," warns us at the outset that we would seriously err if we were to suppose that these references to heavenly councils were figurative rather than literal expressions on the part of the prophets. Another scholar [Edwin C. Kingsbury] observes that the allusions to these heavenly councils were clearly understood by those to whom the prophets originally wrote, and that it has taken a later generation to misunderstand and remove them.

A natural companion to the above-quoted Jeremiah passage is one of our most often quoted [LDS] missionary scriptures, Amos 3:7: "Surely the Lord God will do nothing, but he revealeth his secret unto his servants the prophets." The word "secret" in this text is the same as that found in the marginal reading in Jeremiah. As in Jeremiah, its root is "sod," and again the context is that of heavenly councils. What Amos is telling us is that the Lord doesn't act independently of the heavenly council where all prophets are instructed and ordained. (Premortal Existence, Foreordinations, and Heavenly Councils," pp. 185-186.)

10

Priesthood Authority

Essential Doctrine:

According to the Bible, any church claiming to be the true church of Jesus Christ **must claim to have priesthood authority and authorization to act in the name of God. It must claim that its priesthood holders can trace their authority back to Christ and the apostles of the ancient Christian church.**

Key Bible Passages:

Ex. 18:15-16 (13-26)	The people come unto me to enquire of God. I judge between one and another and make them know the statutes of God, and his laws.
Ex. 28:41 (1-43)	Anoint them, and consecrate them, and sanctify them, that they may minister unto me in the priest's office.
Num. 16:5 (1-35)	The Lord will shew who are his, and who is holy, even he whom he hath chosen.
Num. 27:22-23 (18-23)	Moses set Joshua before the congregation; he laid his hands upon him, and gave him a charge, as the Lord commanded.

Deut. 34:9	Joshua was full of the spirit of wisdom, for Moses had laid his hands upon him.
1 Sam. 3:19-20	Samuel grew, and the Lord was with him. He was established to be prophet.
2 Chron. 26:18 (16-21)	It appertaineth not unto thee, Uzziah, to burn incense unto the Lord, but unto the priests.
Hag. 1:12	The people obeyed the voice of Haggai the prophet, as the Lord their God had sent him.
Matt. 16:19 (13-19)	I will give unto thee the keys of the kingdom, whatsoever thou shalt bind on earth shall be bound in heaven.
Mark 3:14 (13-19)	He ordained twelve, that they should be with him to preach, to heal sicknesses, and to cast out devils.
Mark 11:28 (27-33)	By what authority doest thou these things? and who gave thee this authority to do these things?
Luke 9:1 (1-2)	He called his twelve disciples and gave them power and authority.
Luke 10:1 (1-17)	The Lord appointed other seventy also, and sent them two by two into every place.
John 15:16	Ye have not chosen me, but I have chosen you, and ordained you.
Acts 6:6 (1-6)	The apostles prayed and laid their hands on them.
Acts 8:20 (14-24)	Thy money perish with thee, because thou hast thought the gift of God may be purchased with money.
Acts 13:1-3	When they had fasted and prayed, they laid their hands on them.

Acts 19:5 (1-6)	Paul rebaptized people previously baptized by individuals lacking priesthood authority.
Gal. 1:1	An apostle, not by man, but by Jesus Christ and God the Father.
1 Tim. 4:14	Neglect not the gift that is in thee, which was given thee by prophecy, with the laying on of hands of the presbytery.
Titus 1:5	Ordain elders in every city, as I had appointed thee.
Heb. 5:4	No man taketh this honour unto himself, but he that is called of God, as was Aaron. (See Ex. 28:1,3,41)
Rev. 1:6	Christ hath made us kings and priests unto God and his Father.

References for Further Study:

1. Elaine Pagels, *The Gnostic Gospels*, (New York: Vintage Books, 1979), p. 54.

2. James. L. Barker, *Apostasy From the Divine Church*, (Salt Lake City: Bookcraft, Inc., 1984) p. 132.

3. Hugh Nibley, *Iranaeus*, Farms Preliminary Report (Provo, Utah: Farms, 1984).

4. Bo Reicke, "The Epistles of James, Peter, and Jude," *The Anchor Bible* (Garden City, N.Y.: Doubleday and Company, Inc., 1964), p. 133.

5. G. A. Williamson, translator, *Eusebius: The History of the Church From Christ to Constantine* (Minneapolis, Minnesota: Augsburg Publishing House, 1965), p. 88.

6. See sections 11 and 12 of this book.

Explanatory Notes:

The bishops and apologists of the Early Church stressed the importance of apostolic succession. For them, this was a crucial test of validity. In the ancient Christian church, Peter was considered to be the chief apostle.

Essential to the transmission of priesthood authority is the necessity of one being ordained by one already holding priesthood power, and who is authorized to perform the ordination. Christ ordained his apostles, who in turn ordained other church leaders, thus forming a chain of ordinations. Though the chain was broken and authority was lost through the falling away and great apostasy, three of Christ's apostles returned in the last days to restore the apostleship and higher priesthood to Joseph Smith and Oliver Cowdery. This restored the chain of authority, which again exists unbroken all the way back to Jesus Christ. An authorized priesthood holder can trace his chain of authority back to the Savior.

11

The Melchizedek and Aaronic Priesthoods

Essential Doctrine:

According to the Bible, any church claiming to be the true church of Jesus Christ **must possess the Melchizedek and Aaronic priesthoods.**

Key Bible Passages:

Gen. 14:18	Melchizedek...was the priest of the most high God.
Lev. 3:2	Aaron's sons the priests shall sprinkle the blood upon the altar.
Num. 16:9	The God of Israel hath separated you, to bring you near to himself, to stand before the congregation to minister unto them.
Num. 16:10 (8-11)	And seek ye the priesthood also.
Num. 25:13 (10-13)	He shall have the covenant of an everlasting priesthood; because he was zealous for his God.
Neh. 3:1	Then Eliashib the high priest rose up.
Neh. 13:29 (29-31)	They have defiled the priesthood, and the covenant of the priesthood.
Heb. 5:4	No man taketh this honour unto himself, but he that is called of God, as was Aaron.

Heb. 5:6	Thou art a priest forever after the order of Melchisedec. (7:17)
Heb. 7:5	They that are of the sons of Levi, who receive the office of the priesthood, have a commandment to take tithes of the people.
Heb. 7:11	If perfection were by the Levitical priesthood, what need was there that another priest should rise after the order of Melchisedec, and not be called after the order of Aaron?
Heb. 7:24	Jesus, because he continueth forever, hath an unchangeable priesthood.
1 Pet. 2:9 (5,9)	Ye are a chosen generation, a royal priesthood.

References for Further Study:

1. Richard L. Anderson, *Understanding Paul* (Salt Lake City, Utah: Deseret Book Co., 1983), pp. 208-215.

2. James A. Carver, "Answering an Ex-Mormon Critic," Mormon Miscellaneous Response Series, (Sandy, Utah: Mormon Miscellaneous, 1983), pp. 15-16.

3. John A. Tvedtnes, *The Church of the Old Testament* (Salt Lake City, Utah: Deseret Book Co., 1980), pp. 96-100.

4. See also sections 10 and 12 of this book.

Explanatory Notes:

James Carver says the following:

> Christ was after the Order of Melchizedek. Observe that he was after the Order of Melchizedek. For there to be an order, a group of people must belong. The Greekword for "order" is "taxis," which means, "a fixed succession" or "manner." If Christ belonged to an "order" then Jesus was

not the only one to hold the Melchizedek Priesthood. He established an order of that priesthood in his day. ("Answering An Ex-Mormon Critic," p. 15.)

12

Same Priesthood Offices as Biblical Church

Essential Doctrine:

According to the Bible, any church claiming to be the true church of Jesus Christ **must have the same organization and officers as existed in the primitive church, including prophets, apostles, high priests, seventies, bishops, elders, priests, teachers, and deacons.**

Key Bible Passages:

Gen. 14:18	Melchizedek...was the priest of the most high God.
Ex. 24:9 (1,9-11)	Then went up Moses, and Aaron...and seventy of the elders of Israel.
Deut. 27:1	Moses with the elders of Israel instructed the people to keep the commandments.
Josh. 4:4 (1-4)	Joshua called the twelve men...out of every tribe a man.
Amos 3:7	God revealeth his secret unto his servants the prophets.
Luke 6:13 (12-16)	He chose twelve, whom also he named apostles.
Luke 10:1 (1-3)	The Lord appointed other seventy also.

Acts 1:25 (21-26)	They prayed that he may take part of this ministry and apostleship.
Acts 13:1 (1-3)	There were in the church...prophets and teachers.
Acts 14:23 (21-23)	They ordained them elders in every church.
Acts 15:6 (4-6)	The apostles and elders came together.
Eph. 2:20 (19-21)	The church of God is built upon the foundation of the apostles and prophets.
Eph. 4:11 (11-14)	And he gave some, apostles, and some, prophets, and evangelists, pastors and teachers.
Philip. 1:1	Paul and Timotheus are with the bishops and deacons.
1 Tim. 3:1	If a man desire the office of a bishop, he desireth a good work.
1 Tim. 5:17	Let the elders that rule well be counted worthy of double honor.
Titus 1:5	Ordain elders in every city, as I had appointed thee.
Heb.3:1	Consider the Apostle and High Priest of our profession.
Heb. 5:10	Called of god an high priest after the order of Melchisedec.
Heb. 7:28 (22-28)	For the law maketh men high priests which have infirmity.
Titus 1:7	A bishop must be blameless, as the steward of God.
1 Pet. 5:1-3	The elders which are among you, I exhort.

References for Further Study:

1. See also sections 10 and 11 of this book.

Explanatory Notes:

Paul taught the Corinthians that the church was a carefully organized unit, with *all* parts necessary. He compared the church to the human body. He taught that each part is essential, and that no portion can say to another, "I have no need of thee." (1 Corinthians 12:1-15.) Where in the New Testament were Paul's words ever countermanded? The Savior's church had apostles, prophets, bishops, elders, deacons, etc. How can any church claim to be the Savior's true church and not have apostles and prophets, the two most important offices in the ancient church? It isn't enough to have bishops and deacons but none of the other offices. All of the offices of the ancient Christian church must be found in any organization claiming to be the Savior's true church.

Some churches of today confuse the Biblical offices. For instance, some have come to believe that the office of elder and bishop are the same position. This belief is clearly erroneous. The churches of today should know that not every elder is a bishop, and that a bishop is selected from among the elders of his congregation. This is seen in the writings of the early Christian fathers. For instance, Ignatius, who was himself a bishop, consistently made a distinction between the bishop and the presbytery (the body of elders). In some instances, Ignatius even spoke of the elders helping the bishop (*The Apostolic Fathers*, pp. 78-79, 86, 92, 94-95). For further information on this topic see

1. Daryl Chase, *Christianity Through the Centuries* (Salt Lake City, Utah: Deseret Book Co., 1947), p. 73.

2. James L. Barker, *Apostasy From the Divine Church* (Salt Lake City, Utah: Bookcraft, Inc. 1984), pp. 100-104.

13

An Unpaid Lay Clergy

Essential Doctrine:

According to the Bible, any church claiming to be the true church of Jesus Christ **must have a lay clergy, with only the highest officers being eligible for any type of compensation.**

Key Bible Passages:

Ps. 101:6	He that walketh in a perfect way, he shall serve me.
Isa. 45:13	He shall build my city, not for price nor reward.
Matt. 10:8	Freely have ye received, freely give.
Matt. 20:26-27	Whosoever will be chief among you, let him be your minister, and whosoever will be chief among you, let him be your servant.
Luke 9:23	If any man come after me, let him deny himself, and take up his cross daily, and follow me.
Acts 20:33-34	I have coveted no man's silver, or gold, or apparel.
1 Cor. 4:11-12	Unto this present hour we both hunger and thirst,
1 Cor. 9:18	I preach the gospel of Christ without charge.

2 Cor. 2:17	We are not as many, which corrupt the word of God: but as of sincerity speak we the word of Christ.
2 Cor. 11:7-9	In all things I kept myself from being burdensome unto you, and so will I keep myself.
2 Cor. 12:16-18	I did not burden you...walked we not in the same steps?
Phil. 4:19	God shall supply all your need.
1 Tim. 3:3	Be not greedy of filthy lucre.
1 Peter 5:1-3	Feed the flock of God...willingly...not for filthy lucre.

References for Further Study:

1. Daryl Chase, *Christianity Through the Centuries*, (Salt Lake City, Utah: Deseret Book Co., 1947), p. 31.

2. Bo Reicke, "The Epistles of James, Peter, and Jude," *The Anchor Bible* (Garden City, N.Y., Doubleday and Company, Inc., 1964), p. 128.

3. Jack N. Sparks, ed., *The Apostolic Fathers*, (Nashville: Thomas Nelson Publishers, 1978), p. 316.

4. See also sections 10, 11 and 12 of this book.

Explanatory Notes:

In the primitive church, all officials were unremunerated. As the great apostasy took place, the concept of a paid clergy eventually found its way into the church. In the fourth century bishops began to be salaried, but this was a practice which previously was unacceptable in the Savior's church.

14

The Falling Away

Essential Doctrine:

According to the Bible, any church claiming to be the true church of Jesus Christ **must know that the original church of Christ fell away from the true gospel and embraced false doctrines. The power to act in the name of God was withdrawn from among men, as was gospel knowledge and essential ordinances. Eventually, certainly by no later than the fifth century A.D., the Savior's true church ceased to exist on the earth, and was in existence only in the spirit world.**

Key Bible Passages:

Is. 29:10	The Lord hath poured out upon you the spirit of deep sleep; the prophets and your rulers, the seers hath he covered.
Is. 29:13	This people draw near me with their mouth, and with their lips do honour me, but have removed their heart far from me. (See Matt. 15:7-9, Mk. 7:6-7)
Is. 60:2	Darkness shall cover the earth, and gross darkness the people.
Matt. 13:25 (24-30)	His enemy came and sowed tares among the wheat.
Matt. 23:13	Woe unto you, scribes and Pharisees, ye shut up the kingdom of heaven against men; for ye neither go in yourselves,

	neither suffer ye them that are entering to go in.
Ro. 10:2-3	They have a zeal of God, but not according to knowledge. For they being ignorant of God's righteousness, and going about to establish their own righteousness, have not submitted themselves unto the righteousness of God.
Matt. 24:5	Many shall come in my name, saying, I am Christ, and shall deceive many.
Matt. 24:11	Many false prophets shall rise, and shall deceive many.
John 6:66	Many of his disciples went back, and walked no more with him.
Acts 20:29-30	After my departing shall grievous wolves enter in among you, not sparing the flock. Also of your own selves shall men arise, speaking perverse things, to draw away disciples after them.
1 Cor. 1:11	There are contentions among you.
1 Cor. 3:3	There is among you envying, and strife, and divisions.
2 Cor. 2:17	We are not as many, which corrupt the word of God.
Gal. 1:6-9	I marvel that ye are so soon removed unto another gospel. There are some that trouble you, and would pervert the gospel of Christ.
Gal. 3:1	Who hath bewitched you, that ye should not obey the truth.
2 Thes. 2:2-4	That day (Christ's 2nd Coming) shall not come, except there come a falling away first, and that man of sin be revealed, the son of perdition.
1 Tim. 1:6	Some have turned aside unto vain jangling.

1 Tim. 4:1-3	In the latter times some shall depart from the faith, giving heed to seducing spirits, and doctrines of devils.
2 Tim. 1:15	All they which are in Asia be turned away from me.
2 Tim. 2:18	Who concerning the truth have erred, and overthrow the faith of some.
2 Tim. 3:1-7	In the last days perilous times shall come. Men will have a form of godliness but deny the power thereof.
2 Tim. 4:3-4	The time will come when they will not endure sound doctrine; they shall turn away their ears from the truth, and shall be turned unto fables.
Titus 1:10-16	There are many vain talkers and deceivers, who subvert whole houses, teaching things which they ought not, for filthy lucre's sake.
2 Pet. 2:1-2	There shall be false teachers among you, who shall bring in damnable heresies, even denying the Lord, and many shall follow their pernicious ways.
2 Pet. 3:16-17	They that are unlearned and unstable wrest the scriptures, unto their own destruction.
1 Jn. 2:18	Even now there are many antichrists.
1 Jn. 4:1	Many false prophets are gone out into the world.
Jude 4	Certain men crept in unawares, ungodly men, denying the only Lord God.
Rev. 2:2	Thou hast tried them which say they are apostles, and are not, and hast found them liars.
Rev. 13:7-8	It was given unto him to make war with the saints, and to overcome them, and all that dwell upon the earth shall worship him.

References for Further Study

1. James L. Barker, *Apostasy From the Divine Church* (Salt Lake City: Bookcraft, Inc., 1984).
2. James E. Talmage, *The Great Apostasy* (Salt Lake City, Utah: Deseret Book Co., reprint 1968).
3. Hugh Nibley, *When the Lights Went Out: Three Studies on the Ancient Apostasy* (Salt Lake City: Deseret Book Co., 1976), pp. 1-55.
4. Richard L. Anderson, *Understanding Paul* (Salt Lake City: Deseret Book Co., 1983), pp. 64-65, 85-87, 367-379, 373-378.
5. See section 15 of this book.

Explanatory Notes:

The historical record makes it clear that the Savior's true church ceased to exist after the fifth century A.D. Apostles and prophets were no longer found in the church. Several of the Early Church's most important doctrines—such as pre-mortal existence, man's deification, baptism for the dead, the necessity of good works, and others—were abandoned. The correct understanding of the Godhead being composed of three separate deities was replaced by the unscriptural three-in-one belief.

Scriptures were lost, and those that remained were subjected to uninspired editing. In fact, many of the leaders and theologians of the Reformation and of later Protestantism even admitted that true Christianity had been lost.

Some cite Matthew 16:18, offering it as what they regard as proof that an apostasy did not occur. The passage reads as follows: "And I [Christ] say also unto thee, That thou art Peter, and upon this rock I will build my church; and the gates of hell shall not prevail against it."

How does this verse apply to the apostasy? Does it mean that the falling away was not complete? If so, then what about the numerous New Testament prophecies of an impending apostasy? What about the prophecies concerning a restoration of the gospel? And what about the overwhelming historical evidence that an apostasy did in fact take place?

The correct interpretation of Matthew 16:18 becomes clear when it is understood what the expression "the gates of hell" meant to the Early Church. In early Christian theology, the gates of hell were the entrances to the prison portion of the spirit world. (Nibley, "Baptism for the Dead in Ancient Times" [December 1948], pp. 788, 836; *Harper's Bible Dictionary*, p. 365; cf. Bruce R. McConkie, *Doctrinal New Testament Commentary* [Salt Lake City, Utah: Bookcraft, Inc., 1977], pp. 388-389.) Thus, the Savior was simply saying that Satan would not ultimately triumph over the Church. The gospel was preached in the "spirit prison" while the earth languished in the apostasy of the dark ages. And centuries later Peter, who received the keys of the kingdom, returned from beyond the veil in these latter days to confer those keys upon Joseph Smith, his last days counterpart. Satan and hell did not prevail; the church stands triumphant.

15

The Restoration

Essential Doctrine:

According to the Bible, any church claiming to be the true church of Jesus Christ **must believe that the church and gospel, having previously been taken from the earth, were to be restored in the last days. Therefore, the true church of today must claim to be a restoration of the original true church of Jesus Christ.**

Key Bible Passages

Isa. 2:2 (2-5)	The Lord's house shall be established in the top of the mountains.
Isa. 11:11 (1-16)	The Lord shall set his hand a second time to recover his people.
Is. 29:11-12	The vision of all is become unto you as the words of a book that is sealed.
Isa. 29:14 (1-24)	I will proceed to do a marvelous work among this people, even a marvelous work and a wonder.
Jer. 31:31 (31-34)	I will make a new covenant with the house of Israel, and with the house of Judah.
Ezek. 37:26-27 (11-28)	I will make a new covenant with them; it shall be an everlasting covenant with them. I will be their God, and they shall be my people.

Dan. 2:44
(26-45)
In the days of these kings shall the God of heaven set up a kingdom, which shall never be destroyed.

Mal. 3:1-3
I will send my messenger, and he shall prepare the way, before the Lord shall suddenly come to his temple. (See Luke 7:24-28)

Mal. 4:6
(5-6)
I will send you Elijah the prophet, before the great day of the Lord, and he shall turn the heart of the fathers to the children.

Matt. 17:11
Elias truly shall first come, and restore all things.

Matt. 24:14
The gospel of the kingdom shall be preached in all the world for a witness unto all nations; and then shall the end come.

Acts 3:21-23
The heavens must receive Christ until the times of restitution of all things. A prophet shall the Lord your God raise up unto you.

Rom.11:25
(16-26)
Blindness is happened to Israel until the fulness of the Gentiles be come in.

Eph. 1:10
(9-10)
In the dispensation of the fulness of times he will gather together in one all things in Christ.

Rev. 14:6
(6-7)
I saw another angel fly...having the everlasting gospel to preach to every nation, and kindred, and tongue, and people.

References for Further Study:

1. Richard L. Anderson, *Understanding Paul* (Salt Lake City: Deseret Book Co., 1983), pp. 266-271.

2. Kirk H. Vestal and Arthur Wallace, *The Firm Foundation of Mormonism* (Los Angeles: The LL Co., 1981), pp. 205-211, 233-235.

3. See section 14 of this book.

16

The Church Named after Jesus Christ

Essential Doctrine:

According to the Bible, any church claiming to be the true church of Jesus Christ **must be named after Jesus Christ.**

Key Bible Passages:

Matt. 12:21(16-21) And in his name shall the Gentiles trust.

John 20:31   Believe that Jesus is the Christ, the Son of God; and that believing ye might have life through his name.

Acts 4:12   There is none other name under heaven
(10-12)   given among men, whereby we must be saved.

Ro. 16:16   The churches of Christ salute you.

1 Cor. 6:11 Ye are justified in the name of the Lord
(9-11)   Jesus.

Eph. 5:23-24 Christ is the head of the church: and he is the saviour of the body.

Col. 1:18   He is the head of the body, the church.

Heb. 12:23   The general assembly and church of the firstborn.

1 Jn. 3:23   This is his commandment, that we should believe on the name of his Son Jesus Christ.

References for Further Study:

1. See also sections 15, 17 and 18 of this book.

Explanatory Notes:

With the strong scriptural emphasis concerning salvation resulting through belief in the name of Jesus Christ, it is amazing that almost no other churches except The Church of Jesus Christ of Latterday Saints have the name Jesus Christ as part of their church's name. Latterday Saints were given the name of their church by revelation (D&C 115:34).

Hebrews 12:23 refers to the church as "the church of the fistborn," which is the same as saying "the church of Jesus Christ" since the New Testament speaks of Christ as "the firstborn." (Colossians 1:15,18.)

17

Members Called Saints

Essential Doctrine:

According to the Bible, any church claiming to be the true church of Jesus Christ **must refer to its members as saints.**

Key Bible Passages:

Deut. 33:3 (1-3)	All his saints are in thy hand.
Ps. 50:5	Gather my saints...those that have made a covenant with me by sacrifice.
Dan. 7:18 (18-22)	The saints of the most High shall take the kingdom, and possess the kingdom forever.
Dan. 7:27	The kingdom and dominion shall be given to the people of the saints of the most High.
Zech. 14:5	The Lord my God shall come, and all the saints with thee.
Acts 9:13	How much evil he hath done to thy saints at Jerusalem.
Acts 9:41	He had called the saints and widows.
Rom. 1:7	To all...in Rome, beloved of God, called to be saints.
Rom. 15:26-27	Make a contribution for the poor Saints.
1 Cor. 14:33	God is not the author of confusion, but of peace, as in all churches of the saints.
Eph. 2:19 (19-21)	We are no more strangers...but fellow citizens with the saints.

Eph. 4:11-14	He gave apostles and prophets...for the perfecting of the Saints.
Phili. 1:1-2	To all the saints in Christ Jesus...peace.
Phili. 4:21-23	Salute every saint in Christ Jesus.
Col. 1:2-5	To the saints and faithful brethren in Christ...grace be unto you.
2 Thes. 1:10	He shall come to be glorified in his saints.
Jude 1:14	The Lord cometh with ten thousands of his saints.
Rev. 13:10	Here is the patience and the faith of the saints.

Explanatory Notes:

As can be seen from the scriptural passages cited, faithful followers of the Lord were called saints in both Old and New Testament times, and prophetic passages also refer to church members called saints in the last days.

18

A Missionary Church

Essential Doctrine:

According to the Bible, any church claiming to be the true church of Jesus Christ **must place a strong emphasis on its missionary program and must be a missionary-oriented church.**

Key Bible Passages:

Isa. 2:3 (2-4)	He will teach us of his ways, and we will walk in his paths.
Isa. 61:1 (1-3)	The Lord hath anointed me to preach good tidings.
Jer. 16:16 (14-16)	I will send for many fishers and hunters, saith the Lord, and they shall hunt them from every mountain.
Ezek. 34:11 (11-16)	I will both search my sheep, and seek them out.
Jonah 3:2	Go unto Nineveh, and preach unto it the preaching that I bid thee.
Matt. 4:19 (18-20)	Follow me, and I will make you fishers of men.
Matt. 10:6 (1-20)	But go rather to the lost sheep of the house of Israel.
Matt. 28:19 (19-20)	Go ye therefore, and teach all nations.
Mark 1:4	John did preach the baptism of repentance for the remission of sins.

Mark 3:14	He ordained twelve, that he might send them forth to preach.
Mark 16:15 (15-18)	Go ye into all the world, and preach the gospel to every creature.
Luke 5:10 (2-11)	From henceforth thou shalt catch men.
Luke 9:2 (1-6)	He sent them to preach the kingdom of God.
Luke 22:32 (31-32)	When thou art converted, strengthen thy brethren.
John 4:35 (35-38)	The fields...are white already to harvest.
John 15:16	I have chosen you, and ordained you, that ye should go and bring forth fruit.
John 21:17 (15-17)	Jesus saith unto him, Feed my sheep.
Acts 5:42	They ceased not to teach and preach Jesus Christ.
Acts 10:42 (9-48)	He commanded us to preach unto the people.
Rom. 10:15 (13-17)	How shall they preach, except they be sent?
1 Cor. 9:16 (16-23)	Woe is unto me, if I preach not the gospel.
2 Cor. 4:5	We preach not ourselves, but Christ Jesus the Lord.
2 Tim. 4:2	Preach the word; be instant in season.

19

Continuous Revelation

Essential Doctrine:

According to the Bible, any church claiming to be the true church of Jesus Christ **must believe in the reality and necessity of continuous revelation from God to man.**

Key Bible Passages:

Deut. 29:29	Things which are revealed belong unto us and to our children forever.
1 Kgs. 19:12 (11-15)	And after the fire a still small voice.
Prov. 29:18	Where there is no vision, the people perish.
Dan. 2:29 (28-30)	He that revealeth secrets maketh known...what shall come to pass.
Amos 3:7	Surely the Lord God will do nothing, but he revealeth his secret unto his servants the prophets.
John 10:4	The sheep follow him; for they know his voice.
John 16:13	When he, by the Spirit of truth, is come, he will shew you things to come.
John 17:8	I have given unto them the words which thou gavest me.
Acts 11:12	The Spirit bade me go with them, nothing doubting.
Acts 15:28	It seemed good to the Holy Ghost, and to us,...

Acts 16:6   They were forbidden of the Holy Ghost
                     to preach the word in Asia.
1 Cor. 14:6   I shall speak to you either by revelation
                     or by knowledge.
Eph. 1:17   God...may give unto you the spirit of
(17-18)   wisdom and revelation.
Rev. 19:10   The testimony of Jesus is the spirit of
                     prophecy.

References for Further Study:

1. Richard L. Anderson, *Understanding Paul*, (Salt Lake City, Utah: Deseret Book Co., 1983), pp. 51-53, 66-67, 327-328, 412.
2. See also sections 9 and 12 of this book.

20

More Scripture

Essential Doctrine:

According to the Bible, any church claiming to be the true church of Jesus Christ **must possess additional scripture to supplement the Bible, not to replace it.**

Key Bible Passages:

Isa. 29:11 (11-12)	The vision of all is become as the words of a book that is sealed.
Ezek. 37:16 (15-20)	I will take the sick of Joseph, and put it with the stick of Judah, and make them one stick, and they shall be one in mine hand.
Dan. 12:4 (1-4)	O Daniel, shut up the words, and seal the book, even to the time of the end.
Amos 3:7	Surely the Lord God will do nothing, but he revealeth his secret unto his servants the prophets.
2 Tim. 3:16	All scripture is given by inspiration of God, and is profitable.

References for Further Study:

1. Keith Meservy, "Discoveries at Nimrud and the 'Sticks' of Ezekiel," *Newsletter and Proceedings of the Society for Early Historic Archaeology,* No. 142 (November, 1978), pp. 1-10.

2. "Ezekiel's Sticks," *The Ensign* (September, 1977), pp. 22-27.

3. Kirk Holland Vestal and Arthur Wallace, *The Firm Foundation of Mormonism* (Los Angeles, California: the LL Co., 1981), pp. 45-50.

4. Hugh Nibley, "The Stick of Judah and the Stick of Joseph," *The Improvement Era* (January-May, 1953).

5. See also section 19 of this book.

Explanatory Notes:

In relation to this point, it should be observed that the New Testament Church considered current revelation to be very important. An indication of this comes from the ancient Christian writer Papias, who lived in the early part of the second century and who was the bishop of Hierapolis:

> If anyone chanced to be a fellow of the Elders, I would inquire as to their discourse, what Andrew, or what Peter said, or what Phillip, or what Thomas or James or what John or Matthew or any other of the Lord's disciples [said]....For I did not think that things out of books could profit me so much as the utterances of a voice which liveth and abideth. (From Seaich, *Ancient Texts and Mormonism*, p. 45, quoting Papias from the writings of Eusebius, an early Christian historian of the fourth century; cf. Anderson, *Understanding Paul*, pp. 51-53.)

21

Extra-Biblical Scripture in the Early Church

Essential Doctrine:

According to the Bible, any church claiming to be the true church of Jesus Christ **must know and acknowledge that there have been many more books of scripture than those contained in the present-day Bible.**

Key Bible Passages:

Gen. 5:1	This is the book of the generations of Adam.
Ex. 17:14	Write this for a memorial in a book.
Ex. 24:7	He took the book of the covenant, and read in the audience of the people.
Num. 21:14	It is said in the book of the wars of the Lord.
Jos. 10:13	Is not this written in the book of Jasher?
1 Sam. 10:25	Samuel told the people the manner of the kingdom, and wrote it in a book.
2 Sam. 1:18	It is written in the book of Jasher.
1 Kings 11:41	Are they not written in the book of the acts of Solomon?
1 Chron. 29:29	The acts of David...are written in the book of Samuel the seer, and in the

	book of Nathan the prophet, and in the book of Gad the seer.
2 Chron. 9:29	Are they not written in the book of Nathan the prophet, and in the prophecy of Ahijah the Shilonite, and in the visions of Iddo the seer?
2 Chron. 12:15	Are they not written in the book of Shemaiah the prophet, and of Iddo the seer?
2 Chron. 13:22	The rest of the acts...are written in the story of the prophet Iddo.
2 Chron. 20:34	The rest of the acts...are written in the book of Jehu.
2 Chron. 26:22	The rest of the acts of Uzziah did Isaiah the prophet write.
2 Chron. 33:19	They re written among the sayings of the seers.
1 Cor. 5:9	I wrote unto you in an epistle....
Eph. 3:3	I wrote afore in few words,...
Col. 4:16	When this epistle is read among you, likewise read the epistle from Laodicea.
Jude 3	It was needful for me to write unto you.

References for Further Study:

1. James Barr, *Holy Scripture: Canon, Authority, Criticism* (Philadelphia, Pennsylvania: The Westminster Press, 1983), pp. 1-104.

2. *Beyond Fundamentalism*, (Philadelphia, Pennsylvania: The Westminster Press, 1984), pp. 41-50.

3. Eugene Seaich, *Ancient Texts and Mormonism*, (Sandy, Utah: Mormon Miscellaneous: 1983), pp. 35, 130.

4. Robert F. Pfeiffer, *Introduction to the Old Testament* (New York, New York: Harper and Brothers, Publishers, 1941), p. 66.

5. *Harper's Bible Dictionary*, pp. 110-112.

6. Brooke Foss Westcott, *The Bible in the Church* (Grand Rapids, Michigan: Baker Book House, reprint 1979), pp. 304-312.

7. Ian Wilson, *Jesus: The Evidence* (San Francisco, California: Harper & Row, Publishers, 1984), pp. 12-31.

8. George W. Buchannan, *To the Hebrews*, The Anchor Bible (Garden City, New York: Doubleday and Company,inc., 1972), p. xxvii-xxx.

9. See also section 20 of this book.

Explanatory Notes:

There are many verses where the Bible quotes as scripture sources which are no longer in any Protestant or Catholic canon and which have either been lost or which cannot even be identified. The past existence of these missing scriptures is acknowledged by many scholars. (See, for example, Bo Reicke, *The Epistles of James, Peter and Jude*, pp. 171-172. See also Smith, "Aporias: Alleged Biblical Inconsistencies,, Discrepancies, and Errors" [Provo, Utah: Unpublished manuscript, 1983, available from *Farms*], Appendix C; Morton Smith, *Jesus the Magician* [San Francisco, California: Harper & Row, Publishers, 1978], pp. 96-104, 118-119, 134-135; Pfeiffer, *Introduction to the Old Testament*, p. 66; Barr, *Holy Scripture*, pp. 8, 25, 44-60, 62, 83; *Beyond Fundamentalism*, pp. 41-50; and Achtemeir, *The Inspiration of Scripture*, p. 60.)

The same holds true for the writings of the Apostolic Fathers (e.g. *The Apostolic Fathers*, pp. 31, 62, 65, and 289.)

22

The Church's Authority over Scripture

Essential Doctrine:

According to the Bible, any church claiming to be the true church of Jesus Christ **must claim to possess, and occasionally exercise, the prophetic prerogative to reinterpret, supercede, revise, or provide additional insight about previously-written scripture.**

Key Bible Passages:

Isa. 30:8	Write it, and note it in a book, that it may be for the time to come for ever and ever.
Jer. 36:28	Take thee another roll, and write in it all the former words that were in the first roll, which Jehoiakim hath burned.
Jer. 36:32	Baruch wrote all the words which Jehoiakim had burned, and there were added besides unto them many like words.
Amos 3:7	Surely the Lord God will do nothing, but he revealeth his secret unto his servants the prophets.
Hab. 2:2 (2-3)	Write the vision, and make it plain upon tables.

2 Tim. 3:16   All scripture is given by inspiration of
                   God, and is profitable for doctrine, for
                   reproof, for correction, for instruction
                   in righteousness.

References for Further Study

1. Paul J. Achtemeier, *The Inspiration of Scripture* (Philadelphia, Pennsylvanis: The Westminster Press, 1980), pp. 62-65, 82-93.

2. Markus Barth, *Ephesians 1-3*, The Anchor Bible (Garden City, New York: Doubleday and Company, Inc., 1974), pp. 27-31, 276-282, 472-477.

3. Richard L. Anderson, *Understanding Paul* (Salt Lake City, Utah: Deseret Book Company, 1983), pp. 51-53.

4. Ian Barber, *What Mormonism Isn't, A Response to the Research of Jerald and Sandra Tanner* (Auckland, New Zealand: Pioneer Books, 1981), pp. E/1-E/9.

5. Kirk H. Vestal and Arthur Wallace, *The Firm Foundation of Mormonism*, pp. 33-43.

6. Bo Reicke, *The Epistles of James, Peter, and Jude* The Anchor Bible (Garden City, N.Y.: Doubleday and Company, Inc., 1984), p. 105.

7. See also sections 19, 20 and 21 of this book.

23

The First Principles

Essential Doctrine:

According to the Bible, any church claiming to be the true church of Jesus Christ **must believe that faith, repentance, baptism by immersion for the remission of sins, and receiving the gift of the Holy Ghost by the laying on of hands are essential steps in an individual's acceptance of the benefits of Christ's atoning sacrifice.**

Key Bible Passages:

Faith

Ps. 34:22 (21-22)	The Lord redeemeth the soul of his servants, and none of them that trust in him shall be desolate.
Prov. 3:5 (5-6)	Trust in the Lord with all thine heart.
Matt. 9:29 (27-31)	Then touched he their eyes, saying, According to your faith be it unto you.
Mark 9:23 (14-26)	All things are possible to him that believeth.
Mark 16:16 (15-18)	He that believeth and is baptized shall be saved, but he that believeth not shall be damned.
Luke 7:30	They rejected the counsel of God...being not baptized of him.
John 3:15 (15-18,36)	Whosoever believeth in God's only begotten Son should not perish, but have everlasting life.

John 5:24	He that heareth my word, and believeth on him that sent me, hath everlasting life, and shall not come into condemnation.
John 6:40	Every one which seeth the Son, and believeth on him, may have everlasting life.
John 6:47	He that believeth on me hath everlasting life.
John 11:25 (11-44)	I am the resurrection and the life: he that believeth in me, though he were dead, yet shall he live.
John 20:31	These are written, that ye might believe that Jesus is the Christ, the Son of God; and that believing ye might have life through his name.
Acts 10:43	To him give all the prophets witness, that through his name whoso believeth in him shall receive remission of sins.
Ro. 1:17 (16-17)	Therein is the righteousness of god revealed from faith to faith: as it is written, the just shall live by faith.
James 2:20 (14-26)	Faith without works is dead.

Repentance

Prov. 28:13	He that covereth his sins shall not prosper: but whoso confesseth and forsaketh them shall have mercy.
Isa. 55:7 (6-7)	Let the wicked forsake his way, and the unrighteous man his thoughts, and let him return unto the Lord, and he will have mercy.
Ezek. 18:21 (19-31)	If the wicked will turn from all his sins that he hath committed, and do that which is lawful and right, he shall surely live, he shall not die.

Matt. 4:17	Jesus began to preach, and to say, Repent: for the kingdom of heaven is at hand.
Matt. 9:13 (10-13)	I am not come to call the righteous, but sinners to repentance.
Mark 1:15	Repent ye, and believe the gospel.
Luke 3:8 (1-14)	Bring forth therefore fruits worthy of repentance.
Luke 15:7 (1-10)	Joy shall be in heaven over one sinner that repenteth, more than over ninety and nine just persons, which need no repentance.
Luke 24:47 (45-47)	Repentance and remission of sins should be preached in his name among all nations.
Acts 2:38 (37-38)	Repent, and be baptized every one of you in the name of Jesus Christ for the remission of sins.
Acts 3:19	Repent ye therefore, and be converted, that your sins may be blotted out.
Acts 11:18	Then hath God also to the Gentiles granted repentance unto life.
Acts 17:30	God...now commandeth all men every where to repent.
2 Cor. 7:10 (8-11)	Godly sorrow worketh repentance to salvation not to be repented of.
James 4:8 (8-10)	Cleanse your hands, ye sinners; and purify your hearts, ye double minded.
1 John 1:9 (7-10)	If we confess our sins, he is faithful and just to forgive us our sins, and to cleanse us from all unrighteousness.

Baptism by the Proper Authority is Essential for Salvation

Mark 16:16 (15-16)	He that believeth and is baptized shall be saved; but he that believeth not shall be damned.

Luke 3:3	John came preaching the baptism of repentance for the remission of sins.
Luke 7:30 (28-30)	The Pharisees and lawyers rejected the counsel of God against themselves, being not baptized of him.
John 3:5	Except a man be born of water and of the Spirit, he cannot enter into the kingdom of God.
Acts 8:38 (38-39)	They went down both into the water, both Philip and the eunuch, and he baptized him.
Acts 19:5 (1-6)	They were baptized in the name of the Lord. (Rebaptism of those baptized without proper authority.)
Acts 22:16 (14-16)	Arise, and be baptized, and wash away thy sins, calling on the name of the Lord.
Ro. 6:4 (3-5)	We are buried with him by baptism into death,...that we also should walk in newness of life.
Gal. 3:27	For as many of you as have been baptized into Christ have put on Christ.
Eph. 4:5	One Lord, one faith, one baptism.
Col. 2:12	Buried with him in baptism, wherein also ye are risen with him through the faith of the operation of God.
Titus 3:5	He saved us, by the washing of regeneration, and renewing of the Holy Ghost.
1 Pet. 3:21 (20-21)	Baptism doth also now save us, by the answer of a good conscience toward God.

Confirmation After Baptism:
Receiving the Gift of the Holy Ghost

| 1 Sam. 16:13 | The Spirit of the Lord came upon David from that day forward. |

Luke 1:15	He shall be filled with the Holy Ghost.
Luke 3:16	He shall baptize you with the Holy Ghost and with fire.
John 7:39 (37-39)	This spake he of the Spirit, which they that believe on him should receive.
Acts 1:5	Ye shall be baptized with the Holy Ghost.
Acts 2:38	Repent, and be baptized,...and ye shall receive the gift of the Holy Ghost.
Acts 5:32	The Holy Ghost, whom God hath given to them that obey him.
Acts 10:45 (44-45)	He poured out the gift of the Holy Ghost.
Acts 11:16 (16-17)	Ye shall be baptized with the Holy Ghost.

References for Further Study:

1. Ralph P. Martin, *Worship in the Early Church* (Grand Rapids, Michigan: William B. Eerdmans Publishing Co., 1974), pp. 87-97.

2. James E. Talmage, *The Articles of Faith*, (Salt Lake City, Utah: The Church of Jesus Christ of Latter-day Saints, reprint 1976), pp. 165-167, 179-197.

3. James L. Barker, *Apostasy From the Divine Church*, (Salt Lake City, Utah: Bookcraft Publishing Co., reprinted 1984), pp. 165-174.

4. Richard L. Anderson, *Understand Paul* (Salt Lake City, Utah: Deseret Book Company, 1983), pp. 208-209.

5. Bo Reicke, *The Epistles of James, Peter, and Jude* The Anchor Bible (Garden City, N.Y.: Doubleday and Company, Inc., 1964), pp. 74-75.

6. See also section 19 of this book.

Explanatory Notes:

The necessity of baptism by the proper authority was a firmly established doctrine of the early church. For example, Ignatius stated that no baptism was valid without the bishop's approval:

> It is not right either to baptize or to celebrate the agape apart from the bishop; but whatever he approves is also pleasing to God, so that everything you do may be secure and valid. (*The Apostolic Fathers*, p. 113.)

Cyprian, bishop of Carthage in the middle part of the third century, stated that no one outside of the church could administer a valid baptism. (Jeffrey Burton Russell, *Satan: The Early Christian Tradition* [Ithaca, New York: Cornell University Press, 1981], p. 106).

On the necessity of the ordinance of baptism, Tertullian, known as the first great Latin theologian of ancient Christianity, taught the "sole necessary way" of obtaining Christ's protection against evil was through baptism. (*Ibid.*, pp. 100-101.) In fact, it was universally believed in the Early Church that "we obtain the benefits of Christ's sacrifice by baptism." (*Ibid.*, p. 103.)

Anyone who asserts that baptism is only a nice outward sign and that it is not really essential to salvation is out of harmony with both the Bible and the Early Church.

24

Sabbath Observance

Essential Doctrine:

According to the Bible, any church claiming to be the true church of Jesus Christ **must consider Sunday to be the sabbath, the Lord's day, and observe it as a day of rest and spiritual nourishment. It will hold weekly worship services on this day.**

Key Bible Passages:

Gen. 2:3 (2-3)	God blessed the seventh day, and sanctified it.
Ex. 16:23 (22-30)	Tomorrow is the rest of the holy sabbath unto the Lord.
Ex. 20:8 (8-11)	Remember the sabbath day, to keep it holy.
Ex. 23:12	On the seventh day thou shalt rest, that (you) may be refreshed.
Ex. 31:13 (12-18)	My sabbaths ye shall keep: for it is a sign between me and you throughout your generations.
Ex. 31:17	On the seventh day he rested, and was refreshed.
Deut. 5:12 (12-15)	Keep the sabbath day to sanctify it, as the Lord thy God hath commanded thee.

Isa. 58:13 (13-14)	Turn away from doing thy pleasure on my holy day, and call the sabbath a delight, the holy of the Lord.
Jer. 17:21 (19-27)	Take heed to yourselves, and bear no burden on the sabbath day.
Ezek. 20:12 (12,20)	I gave them my sabbaths, to be a sign between me and them, that they might know that I am the Lord that sanctify them.
Matt. 12:8 (1-12)	For the Son of man is Lord even of the sabbath day.
Mark 2:27 (23-28)	The sabbath was made for man, and not man for the sabbath.
Mark 3:4 (1-6)	Is it lawful to do good on the sabbath days, or to do evil?
Luke 6:5 (1-10)	The Son of man is Lord also of the sabbath.
Acts 13:42	The Gentiles besought that these words might be preached to them the next sabbath.
Acts 18:4	And he reasoned in the synagogue every sabbath.
Acts 20:7	Upon the first day of the week, when the disciples came together to break bread, Paul preached unto them.
Col. 2:16 (16-17)	Let no man judge you...in respect of...sabbath days.
Rev. 1:10	I was in the Spirit on the Lord's day.

References for Further Study:

1. Jack N. Sparks, ed., *The Apostolic Fathers* (Nashville, Tennessee: Thomas Nelson Publishers, 1978), p. 317.

2. Ralph P. Martin, *Worship in the Early Church* (Grand Rapids, 1974), pp. 76-82.

3. LeGrand Richards, *A Marvelous Work and a Wonder* (Salt Lake City, Utah: Deseret Book Company, 1978), pp. 335-339.

4. D. A. Carson, ed., *From Sabbath to Lord's Day: A Biblical, Historical, and Theological Investigation* (Grand Rapids, Michigan: Zondervan Publishing House, 1982).

25

Tithing

Essential Doctrine:

According to the Bible, any church claiming to be the true church of Jesus Christ **must ask its members to obey the law of tithing.**

Key Bible Passages:

Gen. 14:20	Abraham gave tithes of all.
Gen. 28:22	Of all that thou shalt give me I will surely give the tenth unto thee.
Lev. 27:30 (30-32)	All the tithe of the land...is the Lord's: it is holy unto the Lord.
Num. 18:26 (21,24,26)	Offer up an offering for the Lord, even a tenth part.
Deut. 14:22 (22-29)	Thou shalt truly tithe all the increase of thy seed, that the field bringeth forth year by year.
2 Chr. 31:5 (5-6)	The tithe of all things brought they in abundantly.
Prov. 3:9 (7-10)	Honour the Lord with thy substance, and with the firstfruits of all thine increase.
Mal. 3:8	Will a man rob God? Wherein have we robbed thee? In tithes and offerings.
Mal. 3:10 (10-12)	Bring ye all the tithes into the storehouse, and prove me now herewith, saith the Lord, if I will not open you the win-

	dows of heaven and pour you out a blessing.
Matt. 23:23	Ye pay tithe of mint and anise and cum-min, and have omitted the weightier matters of the law, judgment, mercy, and faith.
Luke 18:12	I give tithes of all that I possess.
Heb. 7:2 (1-4)	Abraham gave a tenth part of all.

References for Further Study:

1. James Barker, *Apostasy from the Divine Church* (Salt Lake City, Utah: Bookcraft Publishing Co., reprinted 1984), pp. 76-77.

Explanatory Notes:

On occasion, when instructed to do so by the Lord, the true church of Jesus Christ may also ask its members to have "all things common." See Acts 2:44-47; 4:32-37.

26

The Sacrament

Essential Doctrine:

According to the Bible, any church claiming to be the true church of Jesus Christ **must bless and administer the Sacrament (the Lord's Supper) to its members at one of its Sunday meetings. The Sacrament must be intended only for worthy members of the church.**

Key Bible Passages:

Matt. 26:26 (26-28)	Jesus took bread, and blessed it, and brake it, and gave it to his disciples, and said, Take, eat; this is my body.
Matt. 26:27 (26-29)	He took the cup, and gave thanks, and gave it to them, saying, Drink ye all of it.
Luke 22:15-20	He took the cup and gave thanks. And he took bread, and gave thanks, and brake it, and gave unto them.
Acts. 2:42	They continued stedfastly in the apostles' doctrine and fellowship, and in breaking of bread, and in prayers.
Acts 20:7	Upon the first day of the week, when the disciples came together to break bread, Paul preached unto them.
1 Cor. 11:29 (27-30)	He that eateth and drinketh unworthily, eateth and drinketh damnation.

References for Further Study:

1. Jack N. Sparks, ed., *The Apostolic Fathers* (Nashville, Tennessee: Thomas Nelson Publishers, 1978), pp. 314, 317.

2. Richard L. Anderson, *Understanding Paul* (Salt Lake City, Utah: Deseret Book Co., 1983), pp. 107-109.

3. James L. Barker, *Apostasy From the Divine Church* (Salt Lake City, Utah: Bookcraft Publishing Co., reprinted 1984), pp. 73-76.

4. Ralph P. Martin, *Worship in the Early Church* (Grand Rapids, 1984), pp. 120-129.

Explanatory Notes:

Anderson, Barker, and Martin discuss such things as the Sacrament prayer, the manner in which the Lord's Supper was passed, etc.

27

A Persecuted Church

Essential Doctrine:

According to the Bible, any church claiming to be the true church of Jesus Christ **must be a church which is criticized and persecuted by evil men and organizations.**

Key Bible Passages:

2 Chr. 36:16	They mocked the messengers of God, and despised his words, and misused his prophets.
Lam. 5:5	Our necks are under persecution: we labour, and have no rest.
Matt. 5:10 (10-12)	Blessed are they which are persecuted for righteousness' sake, for theirs is the kingdom of heaven.
Matt. 5:12 (11-12)	Rejoice, for great is your reward in heaven: for so persecuted they the prophets which were before you.
Matt. 13:21	Tribulation or persecution ariseth because of the word.
Mark 4:17	Afterward,...persecution ariseth for the word's sake.
Luke 6:22 (2-23)	Blessed are ye, when men shall hate you, and separate you from their company, and cast out your name as evil, for the Son of man's sake.

Acts 5:41 (40-42)	They rejoiced that they were counted worthy to suffer shame for his name.
Acts 8:1 (1-4)	There was a great persecution against the church which was at Jerusalem.
Ro. 8:17	We are joint-heirs with Christ; if so be that we suffer with him, that we may be also glorified together.
2 Cor. 1:7	As ye are partakers of the sufferings, so shall ye be also of the consolation.
2 Tim. 3:12 (12-13)	All that will live godly in Christ Jesus shall suffer persecution.
Heb. 12:6 (6-7)	Whom the Lord loveth he chasteneth, and scourgeth every son whom he receiveth.
1 Pet. 4:13 (12-16)	Rejoice, inasmuch as ye are partakers of Christ's sufferings; that when his glory shall be revealed, ye may be glad with exceeding joy.

References for Further Study:

1. Robert Wilken, *The Christians As The Romans Saw Them* (London: Yale University Press, 1984).

2. Robin Lane Fox, *Pagans and Christians* (New York, New York: Alfred Knopf, Inc., 1987), pp. 419-492.

28

Cross Not Used

Essential Doctrine:

Any church claiming to be the true church of Jesus Christ **must not use the cross as a religious object, and must recognize that the cross is a pagan symbol which was introduced into the church as part of the great apostasy which led to the dark ages.**

Key Bible Passages:

Matt. 27:32	Him they compelled to bear his cross.
Matt. 27:39-40	They reviled him, wagging their heads, saying, If thou be the Son of God, come down from the cross.
Matt. 27:42	Let him now come down from the cross, and we will believe him.
Mark 15:32	Let Christ the King of Israel descend now from the cross, that we may see and believe. And they reviled him.
Gal. 5:11	Then is the offence of the cross ceased.
Phili. 2:8	(Christ) humbled himself, and became obedient unto death, even the death of the cross.
Heb. 12:2	Jesus endured the cross, despising the shame.

Explanatory Notes:

The early Christians did not consider the cross to be a virtuous symbol, but rather as "the accursed tree," a device of death and shame. (Cf. Hebrews 12:2.) Their faith was in what was accomplished on the cross, but not in the cross itself. Some translators translate the Greek word for "cross" as "torture stick."

The cross was a pagan symbol that predated Christianity by hundreds of years. The early Christians did not use the cross as a religious symbol. Ralph Woodrow, who has done extensive research on this subject, has said the following:

> It was not until Christianity began to be paganized (or, as some prefer, paganism was Christianized), that the cross image came to be thought of as a Christian symbol. It was in 431 that crosses in churches and chambers were introduced, while the use of crosses on steeples did not come until about 586. In the sixth century, the crucifix image was sanctioned by the church of Rome. It was not until the second Council at Ephesus that private homes were required to possess a cross.
>
> According to *An Expository Dictionary of New Testament Words*, the cross originated among the Babylonians of ancient Chaldea: "The ecclesiastical form of a two-beamed cross...had its origin in ancient Chaldea, and was used as the symbol of the god Tammuz (being in the shape of the Mystic Tau, the initial of his name) in that country and in adjacent lands, including Egypt...."
>
> In any book on Egypt that shows the old monuments and walls of the ancient temples, one can see the use of the Tau cross....

The Greeks depicted crosses on the head-band of their god corresponding to Tammuz of the Babylonians. Porcelli mentions that Isis was shown with a cross on her forehead. Her priests carried processional crosses in their worship of her. The temple of Serapis in Alexandria was surmounted by a cross....

"But since Jesus died on a cross," some question, "does this not make it a Christian symbol?" It is true that in most minds the cross has now come to be associated with Christ. But those who know its history and the superstitious ways it has been used—especially in past centuries—can see another side of the coin. Though it sounds crude, someone has asked: "Suppose Jesus had been killed with a shotgun; would this be any reason to have a shotgun hanging from our necks or on top of the church roof?" It comes down to this: The important thing is not what, but who—who it was that died, not what the instrument of death was. St. Ambrose [an early Christian bishop in the fourth century] made a valid point when he said, "Let us adore Christ, our King, who hung upon the wood, and not the wood." (*Babylon Mystery Religion* [Riverside, California: Ralph Woodrow Evangelistic Association, Inc., 1981], pp. 48-52.)

On a related note, according to Vassilios Tzaferis, an archaeologist who has directed several excavations in Israel, prior to the fifth century early Christian artists refrained from drawing scenes of the crucifixion:

Early Christian artists, although frequently representing events from the life of Jesus, refrained from drawing scenes of the crucifixion during the first 500 years of Christian

history. The earliest Christian representation
of the crucifixion dates to the late fifth or early
sixth centuries A.D., i.e., about 200 years after
crucifixion was legally abolished....*Biblical Archaeology Review* [January/February 1985], p.
52.)

One of the most thorough and authoritative books on
early Christian symbolism to be published in recent years
is Graydon Snyder's *AntePacem: Archaeological Evidence of
Church Life Before Constantine* (Macon, Georgia: Mercer
University Press, 1985). In chapter two therein Snyder
argues that the cross was not used as a Christian symbol
until after the time of Constantine, i.e. after the early part
of the fourth century. Snyder refers to the "striking lack of
crosses in early Christian remains."

29

Good Works and Obedience Are Essential

Essential Doctrine:

According to the Bible and the writings of early Christian leaders, any church claiming to be the true church of Jesus Christ **must believe that good works and obedience to God's commandments are essential elements of Christian conduct, and that without them no one can dwell eternally in glory with Heavenly Father. It must believe that faith without works is dead. It must know that more than just a verbal acknowledgment that Christ is one's Savior is required to enable a person to live with Heavenly Father in the hereafter.**

Key Bible Passages:

Gen. 26:5 (4-5)	Abraham obeyed my voice, and kept my charge, my commandments, my statutes, and my laws.
Ps. 28:4	Give them according to their deeds, give them after the work of their hands; render to them their desert.
Jer. 17:10	I the Lord search the heart, I give every man according to his ways, and according to the fruit of his doings.

Micah 6:8	What doth the Lord require of thee, but to do justly, and to love mercy, and to walk humbly with thy God.
Matt. 5:16 (14-16)	Let your light so shine before men that they may see your good works, and glorify your Father which is in heaven.
Matt. 7:12	Whatsoever ye would that men should do to you, do ye even so to them.
Matt. 7:21 (21-27)	Not every one that saith unto me, Lord, Lord shall enter into heaven; but he that doeth the will of my Father which is in heaven.
John 3:21 (20-21)	He that doeth truth cometh to the light, that his deeds may be manifest, that they are wrought in God.
John 9:4	I must work the works of him that sent me.
John 14:15	If ye love me, keep my commandments.
John 14:21	He that hath my commandments, and keepeth them, he it is that loveth me.
Rom. 2:13	For not the hearers of the law are just before God, but the doers of the law shall be justified.
Gal. 6:4	Let every man prove his own work.
Philip. 2:12	Work out your own salvation with fear and trembling.
Heb. 5:8-9	He learned obedience by the things he suffered.
James 1:22 (22-25)	Be ye doers of the word, and not hearers only, deceiving your own selves.
James 2:14	What doth it profit, though a man say he hath faith, and have not works? can faith save him?
James 2:17	Faith, if it hath not works, is dead, being alone.
James 2:18	Shew me thy faith without thy works, and I will shew thee my faith by my works.

James 2:20	But wilt thou know, O vain man, that faith without works is dead?
James 2:22	Seest thou how faith wrought with his works, and by works was faith made perfect?
James 2:26	For as the body without the spirit is dead, so faith without works is dead also.
Rev. 20:12 (12-13)	They were judged, every man according to their works.

References for Further Study:

1. Richard L. Anderson, *Understanding Paul* (Salt Lake City, Utah: Deseret Book Co., 1983), pp. 177-187, 272-276, 355-362.

2. See also section 23 of this book.

Explanatory Notes:

In addition to the clear message of scripture on this point, let us consider what the Apostolic Fathers said about this matter:

1 Clement:

> Let us then obey his most holy and glorious Name and escape the threats against the disobedient uttered long ago by Wisdom, that we may dwell with confidence in his most holy and exalted Name....For as God lives, and the Lord Jesus Christ lives, and the Holy Spirit, the object of faith and hope for the elect, the man who with humility and eager gentleness obeys without regret the righteous commandments of God, this man will be listed and enrolled in the number of those who are saved through Jesus Christ, through

whom be glory to God for ever and ever. Amen. (*The Apostolic Fathers*, pp. 49-50.)

2 Clement (or An Ancient Homily By An Unknown Author):

> He [Christ] himself says, "He who acknowledges me before men, I also will acknowledge before my Father"…in what way do we acknowledge him? By doing what he says and not disobeying his commandments, and by honoring him not only with our lips but "with all our heart and all our mind." For he also says in Isaiah, "This people honors me with their lips, but their heart is far from me."
>
> Let us not merely call him Lord, for this will not save us. For he says, "Not every one that says to me, Lord, Lord, will be saved, but he who does righteousness"….
>
> What assurance have we, if we fail to keep our baptism pure and undefiled, that we shall enter into the kingdom of God? Or who will be our advocate, if we are not found to have holy and righteous deeds? (*The Apostolic Fathers*, pp. 57-58; 183-189.)

Ignatius:

> The tree is manifest from its fruits. So those who profess to belong to Christ will be recognized by what they do. For a deed is not a matter of professing now but of continuing to the end by the power of faith.
>
> Let your baptism serve as a shield, faith as a helmet, love as a spear, endurance as full armor. Your works are your deposits so that you may receive the full sum due you. (*The Apostolic Fathers*, pp. 82, 118.)

Polycarp:

> Knowing that God is not mocked, we ought to walk worthily of his commandment and glory....We must all stand at the judgement seat of Christ and each must give account of himself. So then, let us serve him with fear and reverence as he himself commanded, and the apostles who preached the gospel to us and the prophets who proclaimed beforehand the coming of our Lord; let us be fervent for what is good, abstaining from temptation and false brethren and those bearing hypocritically the name of the Lord, who misled vain men. (*The Apostolic Fathers*, pp. 130, 132.)

The Shepherd of Hermas:

> So beware, you who serve the Lord and have him in your hearts. Do the deeds of God, remembering his commandments and the promises which he promised, and trust him, for he will do them [the promises] if his commandments are observed.
>
> Keep the commandments of the Lord and you will be pleasing to him and be enrolled in the number of those who keep his commandments. (*The Apostolic Fathers*, pp. 207, 213.)

The Epistle of Barnabas:

> The Lord will judge the world impartially. Each man will receive payment in accord with his deeds: if he was good, his righteousness precedes him; if he was wicked, the reward of wickedness goes before him. Thus on no account should we slumber in our sins by relaxing as "those who have been called"...[or

else] the wicked Archon will take advantage of his power over us and push us away from the kingdom of the Lord.

...it is fitting that when one has learned the ordinances of the Lord—as many as have been written—he walks in them. For he who does these things will be glorified in God's kingdom. (*The Apostolic Fathers*, pp. 274, 300.)

Those who assert that faith alone is enough, that works are not essential or important, and that a verbal confession that Christ is our Savior is the only thing we need to be saved in our Heavenly Father's kingdom, are simply out of harmony with the ancient Christian Church. They are teaching "another gospel" which was foreign to the Early Church.

30

The Need for Righteous Living

Essential Doctrine:

According to the Bible, any church claiming to be the true church of Jesus Christ **must believe that its members should live a morally clean life. It must oppose sexual sin.**

Key Bible Passages:

Acts 15:29	Abstain...from fornication, from which if ye keep yourselves, ye shall do well.
Rom. 1:26-27	Men burned in their lust one toward another.
Rom. 6:4 (4-6)	We should walk in newness of life.
Rom. 12:1	Present your bodies a living sacrifice, holy, acceptable unto God.
Rom. 13:9	Thou shalt not commit adultery.
Gal. 5:19-21	Now the works of the flesh are...adultery, fornication, uncleanness, lasciviousness, etc.
Col 3:5 (5-10)	Mortify...fornication, uncleanliness, inordinate affection, etc.
1 Thes. 4:3-8	Abstain from fornication. Every one should possess his vessel in sanctification and honour.

References for Further Study:

1. Jack N. Sparks, ed., *The Apostolic Fathers* (Nashville, Tennessee: Thomas Nelson Publishers, 1978), pp. 285-286, 298, 309-310.

31

Spiritual Gifts

Essential Doctrine:

According to the Bible, any church claiming to be the true church of Jesus Christ **must possess spiritual gifts such as prophecy, healing, etc.**

Key Bible Passages:

Amos 7:15 (14-16)	The Lord said unto me, Go, prophesy unto my people Israel.
Mark 16:16-18	These signs shall follow them that believe; in my name shall they cast out devils, speak with new tongues, heal the sick.
Acts 2:4-7	They were all filled with the Holy Ghost, and began to speak with other tongues, as the Spirit gave them utterance.
1 Cor. 12:4-10	There are diversities of gifts, but the same Spirit. Knowledge, faith, healing, miracles, prophecy, tongues, etc.
1 Cor. 13:2 (1,2)	I have the gift of prophecy.
1 Cor. 14:1	Desire spiritual gifts...that ye may prophesy.
1 Cor. 14:3 (1-4)	He that prophesieth speaketh unto men to edification.
1 Cor. 14:5	I would...rather that ye prophesied.
1 Thess. 5:19-20	Quench not the spirit. Despise not prophesyings.

1 Tim. 4:14	Neglect not the gift that is in thee...given
(14-16)	thee by prophecy.
2 Tim. 1:6	Stir up the gift of God.

References for Further Study:

1. James E. Talmage, *The Articles of Faith* (Salt Lake City, Utah: The Church of Jesus Christ of Latterday Saints, reprint, 1976), pp. 217-235.

Explanatory Notes:

Origen noted that in his day there were still a few "prophets and wonders" in the church. He cited this as evidence for Christianity.

32

Higher Teachings and Ordinances

Essential Doctrine:

According to the Bible and to early Christian writers, any church claiming to be the true church of Jesus Christ **must believe that there are special ordinances and teachings, not fully explained in the scriptures, which are reserved for only the most faithful saints. These are usually administered and taught in sacred temples erected especially for this purpose.**

Key Bible Passages:

Allusions to the Temple Service

Rev. 1:6   And hath made us kings and priests unto God and his Father.

Rev. 2:17   To him that overcometh will I give to eat of the hidden manna, and will give him a white stone, and in the stone a new name written, which no man knoweth saving he that receiveth it.

Rev. 3:4-5   Thou hast a few names even in Sardis which have not defiled their garments; and they shall walk with me in white: for they are worthy. He that overcometh, the same shall be clothed in

	white raiment; and I will not blot out his name out of the book of life.
Rev. 3:12	Him that overcometh will I make a pillar in the temple of my God, and I will write upon him the name of my God,...and I will write upon him my new name.
Rev. 3:21	To him that overcometh will I grant to sit with me in my throne.
Rev. 7:2-3	I saw another angel having the seal of the living God, saying, Hurt not the earth,...till we have sealed the servants of our God in their foreheads.
Rev. 7:15	Therefore are they before the throne of God, and serve him day and night in his temple.

Allusions to the Mystery of God

Ro. 16:25	Stablish you according to my gospel, and the preaching of Jesus Christ, according to the revelation of the mystery, which was kept secret since the world began.
1 Cor. 2:7	We speak the wisdom of god in a mystery, even the hidden wisdom, which God ordained before the world unto our glory.
1 Cor. 4:1	Let a man so account of us, as of the ministers of Christ, and stewards of the mysteries of God.
Col. 2:2-3	Being knit together in love, and unto all riches of the full assurance of understanding, to the acknowledgement of the mystery of God, and of the Father, and of Christ. In whom are hid all the treasures of wisdom and knowledge.

1 Tim. 3:8-9   Likewise must the deacons be grave, holding the mystery of the faith in a pure conscience.

Rev. 10:7   In the days of the voice of the seventh angel, the mystery of God should be finished, as he hath declared to his servants the prophets.

References for Further Study:

1. Hugh Nibley, *When the Lights Went Out: Three Studies on the Ancient Apostasy* (Salt Lake City, Utah: Deseret Book Co., 1976), pp. 33-55.

2. Hugh Nibley, *The World and the Prophets* (Salt Lake City, Utah: Deseret Book Co., 1974), pp. 57-64, 149-156.

3. Hugh Nibley, "The Early Christian Prayer Circle," *BYU Studies* (Fall 1976), pp. 41-78.

4. Hugh Nibley, *Since Cumorah* (Salt Lake City, Utah: Deseret Book Co., 1976), pp. 69-126.

5. Hugh Nibley, "Secrecy in the Primitive Church,"*The Improvement Era* (April to June 1965).

6. Hugh Nibley, "What is a Temple?" Brigham Young University, Religious Studies Center, 1984), pp. 19-38.

7. Eugene Seaich, *Ancient Texts and Mormonism*, 56-74; *Mormonism, The Dead Sea Scrolls, and the Nag Hammadi Texts*, pp. 32-49.

8. C. Wilfred Griggs, "The Origin and Formation of the Corpus of Apocryphal Literature," in *Apocryphal Writngs and the Latter-day Saints* , (Provo, Utah: Brigham Young University, Religious Studies Center, 1978), pp. 35-51.

9. Roger J. Adams, *The Iconography of Early Christian Initiation*, Church Educational System Special Project (Salt Lake City, Utah: Unpublished Manuscript, 1977).

10. Blake Ostler, "Clothed Upon: A Unique Aspect of Christian Antiquity," *BYU Studies* (Winter 1982), pp. 31-45.

11. Marcus Von Wellnitz, "The Catholic Liturgy and the Mormon Temple," *BYU Studies* (Winter 1981), pp. 3-35.

Explanatory Notes:

When the pagan critic Celsus accused the early Christians of secrecy, Origen freely admitted that the Early Church had secret doctrines, and he defended their existence:

> "...that there should be certain doctrines, not made known to the multitude, which are revealed after the exoteric [public] ones have been taught, is not a peculiarity of Christianity alone, but also of philosophic systems, in which certain truths are exoteric and others esoteric [confidential, limited to a select few]. Some of the hearers of Pythagora were content with his 'ipse dixit'; while others were taught in secret those doctrines which were not deemed fit to be communicated to profane and insufficiently prepared ears. Moreover, all the mysteries that are celebrated throughout Greece and barbarous countries, although held in secret, have no discredit thrown upon them, so that it is in vain that he [Celsus] endeavors to calumniate [slander] the secret doctrines of Christianity, seeing he does not correctly understand its nature." (*The Ante-Nicene Fathers,* Vol. 4, p. 399.)

Clement of Alexandria (150-215 A.D.) was an elder and a prominent scholar in the Early Church. Under Clement, the Christian school at Alexandria became one of the most outstanding schools of the eastern branch of the ancient Christian church. Historian Frank N. MaGill has given us the following interesting analysis of Clement's teachings on the early Christian gospel:

> Clement concedes that the Scriptures open salvation to the many, who experience the 'first saving change,' when they pass from

heathenism to faith, or from law to Gospel.
But these are saved only in the first degree.
Besides his public teaching, Christ also taught
his Apostles the gnosis [sacred knowledge]
which leads to perfection. This knowledge,
Clement claims, 'has descended by transmission to a few, having been imparted unwrit-
ten by the apostles.' Great preparation and
previous training are necessary to receive it.
But those who can obey it achieve here and
now a foretaste of eternal bliss, and, in the
world to come, will take their places with the
Apostles in the highest sphere. (*Masterpieces
of Christian Literature* (New York: Harper &
Row, Publishers 1963), p. 47.

Ian Barber has made some relevant observations on the
subject under discussion:

...important pieces of Jewish/Christian
literature, such as the Ethiopian text, "The
Combat of Adam and Eve against Satan," in-
troduce elements that have relevance not only
to the theological instruction of the [Mormon
temple] endowment ceremony, but to
material found in such LDS sources as the
Book of Moses (e.g. in "The Combat...") Satan
continually tries to intimidate and confront
Adam while he and Eve offer sacrifice in
similitude of the true sacrifice of Christ. God
sends heavenly messengers to comfort them,
including three messengers who bring "the
signs of the priesthood and Kingship," which
are signs of the atonement to come, as Nibley
summarizes. (See *Nibley on the Timely and the
Timeless*, pp. 2-19)....

It [the fact that there were secret teachings
in the Early Church] goes back to the earliest
Patristic writers, and is stated clearly by

Eusebius [an early Christian historian, 160-339 A.D.], Irenaeus [an ancient bishop and apologist, 115-200 A.D.], and Ignatius [another Early Church bishop, 35-107 A.D.]. Indeed, gnosis is an authentic New Testament Greek word meaning sacred knowledge, and as Nibley points out,....there was a....gnosis centered like the Mormon endowment around the living Christ. It was this that Eusebius asserted the Lord gave secretly to Peter, James, and John in a post-resurrectional setting....In [an article] in the prestigious religious journal *Vigiliae Christinae* (reprinted in *When the Lights Went Out*), Nibley notes that ...a consistently organic body of material argues for the authenticity of a true post-resurrectional gnosis, as Eusebius suggested, involving sacred ordinances. (*What Mormonism Isn't: A Response to the Research of Jerald and Sandra Tanner* (Auckland, New Zealand: Pioneer Books, 1981), pp. H/1-H/2.)

33

Eternal Marriage

Essential Doctrine:

According to the Bible, any church claiming to be the true church of Jesus Christ **must believe that men and women can be married for all eternity.**

Key Bible Passages:

Gen. 2:18	God said, it is not good that the man should be alone; I will make him an help meet for him.
Gen. 2:24 (18,23-24)	Therefore shall a man leave his father and his mother, and shall cleave unto his wife: and they shall be one flesh.
Eccl. 3:14	Whatsoever God doeth, it shall be for ever.
Matt. 16:19	Whatsoever thou shalt bind on earth shall be bound in heaven.
Matt. 19:5 (3-6)	For this cause shall a man leave father and mother, and shall cleave to his wife: and they twain shall be one flesh.
1 Cor. 11:11	Neither is the man without the woman, neither the woman without the man, in the Lord.
Eph. 5:31 (22-33)	For this cause shall a man leave his father and mother, and shall be joined unto his wife, and they two shall be one flesh.

References for Further Study:

1. Eugene Seaich, *Ancient Texts and Mormonism* (Sandy, Utah: Mormon Miscellaneous, 1983), pp. 75-83, 136-140.

2. Eugene Seaich, *Mormonism, the Dead Sea Scrolls, and the Nag Hammadi Texts* (Murray, Utah: Sounds of Zion, 1980), pp. 32-47.

3. *A Great Mystery* (Sandy, Utah: Unpublished manuscript, 1979).

4. LeGrand Richards, *A Marvelous Work and a Wonder* (Salt Lake City, Utah: Deseret Book Co., 1978), pp. 188-201.

5. See section 32 of this book.

Explanatory Notes:

Seaich and Richards demonstrate that there is no contradiction between this doctrine and Matthew 23:23-30. Seaich presents evidence for this doctrine from scriptural and other ancient sources, such as 1 Enoch, a highly regarded text in the Early Church.

34

Baptism for the Dead

Essential Doctrine:

According to the Bible, any church claiming to be the true church of Jesus Christ **must practice the ordinance of baptism for the dead, whereby living individuals are baptized on behalf of those who did not have that opportunity during their mortal lifetimes.**

Key Bible Passages:

Zech. 9:11   By the blood of thy covenant I have sent forth thy prisoners out of the pit wherein is no water. (See 1 Pet. 3:19-20; Is. 24:22;16:1.)

1 Cor. 15:29   Else what shall they do which are baptized for the dead, if the dead rise not at all? why are they then baptized for the dead?

References for Further Study:

1. Duane S. Crowther, *Life Everlasting* (Salt Lake City, Utah: Bookcraft, Inc., 1967), pp. 181-227.

2. Hugh Nibley, "Baptism for the Dead in Ancient Times," *The Improvement Era* (December, 1948 to April, 1949).

3. Robert Millet and Joseph Fielding McConkie, *The Life Beyond* (Salt Lake City, Utah: Bookcraft, Inc., 1986), pp. 165-166.

4. Edward T. Jones, "A Comparative Study of Ascension Motifs in World Religions," in Spencer Palmer, ed., *Diety and Death* (Provo, Utah: Brigham Young University, Religious Studies Center, 1978), p. 86.

5. See also sections 32 and 33 of this book.

Explanatory Notes:

Anderson has said the following concerning 1 Corinthians 15, the resurrection, and baptism for the dead:

> "How do some among you say that there is not resurrection of the dead?" (1 Cor. 15:12, NKJB). Paul's whole discussion centers around this clear question and one other. Reminding the Saints of the certainty of Christ's resurrection, he asks how one could believe in that without believing in the resurrection of mankind. Before the Gospels were written, Paul lists resurrection appearances to leading apostles, to all the apostles, and to "above five hundred brethren at once," most of whom were still alive (1 Cor. 15:6)....We are not "false witnesses," he insists (1 Cor. 15:15). He is not accusing the Corinthians of doubting Christ's resurrection, but jolting them with its reality for consistency's sake. That is the key to the chapter, for doctrines of salvation turn to jarring contradictions if they do not include the resurrection of mankind. If "there is not resurrection" (1 Cor. 15:12)—"if the dead rise not" (1 Cor. 15:15), then the central realities fail. And Paul lists them in order: (1) Christ's own resurrection (1 Cor. 15:13); (2) the apostles' integrity (1 Cor. 15:15); (3) forgiveness through Christ (1 Cor. 15:17); (4) the value of baptisms for the dead (1 Cor. 15:29); (5) the value of Paul's sacrifices and

risks (1 Cor. 15:30-32). This perspective is critical in understanding baptism for the dead, for many commentators toss it aside as a local practice that Paul did not accept. Such an argument is simply near-sighted—the other four points on the above list are not only true but interlocked in Christ's plan of salvation. Baptism for the dead cannot be moved from its rightful relationship by skeptics' shrugs....Thus, baptism for the dead is not incidental to Paul's argument. Nor is it casually thrown into the chapter....Most of the recent translations change "baptized for the dead" to "baptized on behalf of the dead," supporting Joseph Smith's revelations on the subject. (*Understanding Paul*, pp. 125-127.)

Nibley has said the following regarding Paul's reference to baptism for the dead in 1 Corinthians 15:29:

He [Paul] certainly does not cite a practice which he condemns, for that, of course, would weaken his argument: if baptism for the dead is wrong, why should it be cited to strengthen that faith in the resurrection which it illustrates? Oecumenius [a sixth-century Patristic theologian] even suggests that Paul says "why do *they* baptize for the dead" instead of "why do *you*" for fear of offending his hearers and possibly causing them to give up the practice....

Who in the church performed the actual ordinance of baptizing for the dead? It was "those apostles and teachers" of the first generation according to the Shepherd of Hermas, who "went down living into the water" in behalf of those who had died,...("Baptism for the Dead in Ancient Times" [February 1949], pp. 109-110.)

Robert Millet and Joseph Fielding McConkie discuss an Old Testament foreshadowing of baptism for the dead:

> The knowledge that the gospel was to be taught to all, either in this life or the next, and that vicarious ordinances were to be performed for those unable to receive them in earth life, was known to the ancient Saints. There are scriptural, apocryphal, and historical references that evidence that these principles were understood anciently....[A scriptural example]...is found in this prophetic statement by Zechariah: "By the blood of thy covenant I have sent forth thy prisoners out of the pit wherein is no water" (Zechariah 9:11). The pit [also called "prison"] is the spirit world [cf. 1 Peter 3:19-20; Isaiah 24:22; 61:1; Jamieson, Fausset, Brown, in *The Bethany Parallel Commentary on the Old Testament*, Minneapolis, Minnesota: Bethany House Publishers, 1985, pp. 1395, 1495; Roger S. Boraas, in *Harper's Bible Dictionary*, p. 800], but what waters are necessary to free one from captivity? Why, the waters of vicarious baptism—a doctrine taught by Paul and restored through the Prophet Joseph Smith. (*The Life Beyond*, pp. 156-158.)

35

Infant Baptism Not Practiced

Essential Doctrine:

According to the Bible, any church claiming to be the true church of Jesus Christ **cannot believe in baptizing infants before they reach the age of acountability.**

Key Bible Passages:

Matt. 28:29-20	Go and teach all nations, baptizing them: Teaching them to observe all things whatsoever I have commanded you.
Mark 10:13-16	Suffer the little children to come unto me, and forbid them not; for of such is the kingdom of God. (See also Matt. 19:13-15.)
Mark 16:15-16	Go ye into all the world, and preach the gospel to every creature. He that believeth and is baptized, shall be saved; but he that believeth not, shall be damned.
Acts 2:37-39	Repent and be baptized every one of you in the name of Jesus Christ, for the remission of sins, and ye shall receive the gift of the Holy Ghost.

Acts 8:12	They were baptized, both men and women.
Acts 10:34-35	God is no respecter of persons: But in every nation he that feareth Him, and worketh righteousness, is accepted with him.
1 Cor. 7:14	Little children are holy.
1 Cor. 15:22	For as in Adam all die, even so in Christ shall all be made alive. (See also John 5:28-29, and Revelation 20:12-15.)

References for Further Study:

1. James L. Barker, *Apostasy From the Divine Church* (Salt Lake City, Utah: Bookcraft Publishing Co., reprinted 1984), pp. 175-185.

2. James E. Talmage, *The Articles of Faith* (Salt Lake City, Utah: The Church of Jesus Christ of Latter-day Saints, reprint 1976), pp. 125-127.

3. See also sections 23, 30 and 34 of this book.

Explanatory Notes:

The passages cited make it clear that new born infants are not yet eligible for baptism. They are not yet old enough to be taught to observe God's commandments, nor to believe the gospel, nor to sin, nor to repent. Infant children are sanctified through the atonement of Christ, so baptism is not required of them. When they have grown to the age of accountability (typically at age eight), then they have the capacity to meet these prerequisites and to receive the ordinance of baptism.

36

The Savior's Spirit World Ministry

Essential Doctrine:

According to the Bible, any church claiming to be the true church of Jesus Christ **must know that the Savior went as a spirit to the spirit world to preach the gospel immediately after His crucifixion. It must believe that all mankind, whether while in mortality or after death while residing in the spirit world, will have the opportunity to hear and accept the true gospel of Jesus Christ.**

Key Bible Passages:

Zech. 9:11	By the blood of thy covenant I have sent forth thy prisoners out of the pit wherein is no water. (See 1 Pet. 3:19-20; Is. 24:22; 61:1.
John 5:25	The hour is coming, when the dead shall hear the voice of the Son of God: and they that hear shall live.
1 Pet. 3:18-20	Christ went and preached unto the Spirits in prison; which sometime were disobedient.
1 Pet. 4:6	For for this cause was the gospel preached also to them that are dead, that they might be judged according to men in

the flesh, but live according to God in the spirit.

References for Further Study:

1. Duane S. Crowther, *Life Everlasting* (Salt Lake City: Utah: Bookcraft, Inc., 1967), pp.73-105, 181-227.

2. Robert Millet and Joseph Fielding McConkie, *The Life Beyond* (Salt Lake City, Utah: Bookcraft, Inc., 1986), pp. 155-165.

3. Richard L. Anderson, *Understanding Paul* (Salt Lake City, Utah: Deseret Book Co., 1983), pp. 214, 406-407.

4. James L. Barker, *Apostasy From the Divine Church* (Salt Lake City, Utah: Bookcraft Publishing Co., reprinted 1984), p. 63.

5. Claude H. Thompson, "The First Letter of Peter," *The Interpreter's One-Volume Commentary on the Bible*, p. 929.

6. Edward T. Jones, "Comparative Study of Ascension Motifs in World Religions," in Spencer J. Palmer, ed., *Deity and Death* (Provo, Utah: Brigham Young University, Religious Studies Center, 1978), pp. 79-87; cf. pp. 89-99.

7. See also sections 34 and 35 of this book.

Explanatory Notes:

Origen, one of the greatest theologians of the Early Church, stated the following:

> But whether he [Celsus, a pagan critic] likes it or not, we assert that not only while Jesus was in the body did He win over not a few persons merely, but so great a number, that a conspiracy was formed against Him on account of the multitude of His followers; but also, that when He became a soul, without the covering of the body, He dwelt among those souls which were without bodily covering, converting such of them as were willing

> to Himself,...("Against Celsus," *The Ante-Nicene Fathers,* Vol. 4, p. 448.)

Christ was not the only one who taught the gospel in the spirit world. According to the Shepherd of Hermas, Origen, and Hippolytus, the apostles and others also proclaimed the gospel in the spirit world. (Anderson, *Understanding Paul,* p. 214; Seaich, *Ancient Texts and Mormonism,* p. 66.)

The Savior's visit and preaching to those in the prison part of the spirit world came to be known as His "descent into hell."

In speaking of this event and how it was viewed in the Early Church, Jeffrey Burton Russell of the University of California at Santa Barbara has said the following:

> By the second century the belief [in the descent] had already become the most widespread and popular explanation of what Christ was doing between his crucifixion on Friday afternoon and his resurrection on Sunday morning....The descent, like the scourging and the crucifixion itself, was part of the redemptive act....Christ's descent into hell was an important part of the idea of redemption,...For the most part,...the descent into hell became a vehicle for a theology that embraced both justice and mercy. Since God had delayed the Incarnation for centuries after original sin, millions of human beings might have been deprived of an opportunity of salvation solely because they happened to have lived and died before Christ came. The idea of such an injustice was scandalous, and the Christian community sought a way to extend salvation to both the living and the dead. (*Satan: The Early Christian Tradition,* pp. 118-119.)

Russell then summarizes the early Christian answer to this potential injustice:

> If the act of salvation included the descent, and if during the descent Christ preached to those who had died previously, then the effects of redemption could be felt by all. (p. 119.)

37

All Mankind Will
Be Resurrected

Essential Doctrine:

According to the Bible, any church claiming to be the true church of Jesus Christ **must believe that all mankind will be resurrected.**

Key Bible Passages:

Deut. 32:39	I kill, and I make alive; I wound, and I heal.
1 Sam 2:6	The Lord killeth, and maketh alive: he bringeth down to the grave, and bringeth up.
Job 19:26 (25-27)	Though worms destroy this body, yet in my flesh shall I see God.
Ps. 16:9 (9-10)	My flesh also shall rest in hope. For thou wilt not leave my soul in hell.
Isa. 25:8	He will swallow up death in victory; and the Lord God will wipe away tears from all faces.
Isa. 26:19	Thy dead men shall live. Together with my dead body shall they arise.
Ezek. 37:12 (1-14)	I will open your graves, and cause you to come up out.

Dan. 12:2 (1-3)	Many of them that sleep in the dust of the earth shall awake, some to everlasting life.
Hosea 13:14	I will ransom them from the power of the grave; I will redeem them from death.
Matt. 27:52 (52-53)	The graves were opened; and many bodies of the saints which slept arose, and came out of the graves.
Matt. 28:6 (1-20)	He is not here; for he is risen, as he said.
John 5:21	The Father raiseth up the dead, and quickeneth them; even so the Son quickeneth whom he will.
John 6:54 (35-54)	I will raise him up at the last day.
John 11:25 (25-26)	Jesus said...I am the resurrection and the life: he that believeth in me, though he were dead, yet shall he live.
1 Cor. 15:21 (1-58)	Since by man came death, by man came also the resurrection of the dead.
2 Cor. 1:9	Trust...in God which raiseth the dead.
1 Thes. 4:16 (13-17)	The dead in Christ shall rise first.
Rev. 1:18	I am he that liveth, and was dead; and, behold, I am alive for evermore.
Rev. 20:12	I saw the dead, small and great, stand before God;...and the dead were judged.

References for Further Study:

1. James L. Barker, *Apostasy From the Divine Church* (Salt Lake City, Utah: Bookcraft Publishing Co., reprinted 1984), p. 68.

2. See also section 38 of this book.

Explanatory Notes:

Among other evidences for this point, Barker notes that Justin Martyr, a highly esteemed second-century apologist of the Early Church who was put to death by the Romans because he would not deny his testimony of Christ, made reference to the resurrection "of all mankind."

38

Different Degrees of Glory in Heaven

Essential Doctrine:

According to the Bible, any church claiming to be the true church of Jesus Christ **must believe that there will be various degrees of glory in the hereafter.**

Key Bible Passages:

John 14:1-3	In my Father's house are many mansions. I go to prepare a place for you.
1 Cor. 15:40-41	There are celestial bodies, and bodies terrestrial: but the glory of the celestial is one, and the glory of the terrestrial is another. There is one glory of the sun, and another glory of the moon, and another glory of the stars.
2 Cor. 3:18 (17-18)	We are changed into the same image from glory to glory.
2 Cor. 12:2	I knew a man in Christ,...such an one caught up to the third heaven.
Rev. 22:14-15	Blessed are they that do his commandments, and may enter in through the gates into the city. For without are sorcerers, and whoremongers, and murderers, and idolaters, and whosoever loveth and maketh a lie.

_____ , "The Early Christian Prayer Circle," Provo, Utah: *BYU Studies*, Fall 1978, pp.41-78.

_____ , "The Stick of Judah and the Stick of Joseph," *The Improvement Era*, January to May, 1953.

_____ , "Treasures in the Heavens," in Truman Madsen, ed., *Nibley on the Timely and the Timeless*, Provo, 1978, pp. 49-84.

_____ , "What Is A Temple?" in Truman Madsen, ed., *The Temple in Antiquity*, Provo, Utah: Brigham Young, 1984, pp. 19-38.

_____ , *When the Lights Went Out: Three Studies on the Ancient Apostasy*, Salt Lake City, Utah: Deseret Book Co., 1976.

Norman, Keith, "Divinization: The Forgotten Teaching of Early Christianity," *Sunstone*, Winter 1975, pp. 15-19.

_____ , "Ex Nihilo: The Development of the Doctrines of God and Creation in Early Christianity," *BYU Studies*, Spring 1977, pp. 291-318.

Ostler, Blake, "Clothed Upon: A Unique Aspect of Christian Antiquity," *BYU Studies*, Winter 1982, pp. 31-45.

Pagels, Elaine, *The Gnostic Gospels*, New York: Vintage Books, 1979.

Reicke, Bo, *The Epistles of James, Peter, and Jude*, The Anchor Bible, Garden City, N.Y.: Doubleday and Company, Inc., 1964.

Richards, LeGrand, *A Marvelous Work And A Wonder*, Salt Lake City, Utah: Deseret Book Co., 1978.

Richardson, Cyril C., *Early Christian Fathers*, New York: Macmillan Publishing Co., Inc., 1970.

Robinson, H. Wheeler, "The Council of Yahweh," *Journal of Biblical Literature*, Vol. 45, 1944, pp. 151-157.

Russell, Jeffrey Burton, *Satan: The Early Christian Tradition*, Ithaca, 1981.

Seaich, Eugene, *Ancient Texts and Mormonism*, Sandy, Utah: Mormon Miscellaneous, 1983.

_____ , *Mormonism, the Dead Sea Scrolls, and the Nag Hammadi Texts*, Murray, Utah: Sounds of Zion, 1980.

Smith, Morton, *Jesus the Magician*, San Francisco: Harper and Row, Publishers, 1978.

Smith Robert F., "Aporias: Alleged Biblical Inconsistencies, Discrepencies and Errors," Provo, Utah: Unpublished Manuscript, 1983.

_____ , "Satan: Notes on the Gods," Provo, 1986.

Snyder, Graydon, *Ante-Pacem: Archaeological Evidence of Church Life Before Constantine*, Macon, Ga.: Mercer University Press, 1985.

Sparks, Jack N., ed., *The Apostolic Fathers*, Nashville: Thomas Nelson Publishers, 1978.

Talmage, James E., *The Articles of Faith*, Salt Lake City, Utah: The Church of Jesus Christ of Latter-day Saints, reprint 1976.

Turner, Rodney, "The Doctrine of Godhood in the New Testament," in *Principles of the Gospel in Practice*, 1985 Sperry Symposium, Salt Lake City: Randall Book Co., pp. 21-38.

Tvedtnes, John A., *The Church of the Old Testament*, Salt Lake City, Utah: Deseret Book Co., 1980.

Tzaferis, Vassilios, "Crucifixion—The Archaeological Evidence," *Biblical Archaeology Review*, January/February 1985, p. 52.

Vestal, Kirk Holland and Arthur Wallace, *The Firm Foundation of Mormonism*, Los Angeles: The LL Co., 1981.

Wellnitz, Marcus Von, "The Catholic Liturgy and the Mormon Temple," *BYU Studies*, Winter 1981, pp. 3-35.

Wilken, Robert, *The Christians As The Romans Saw Them*, London: Yale University Press, 1984.

Wilson, Ian, *Jesus: The Evidence*, San Francisco: Harper and Row, Publishers, 1984.

Woodrow, Ralph, *Babylon Mystery Religion*, Riverside, 1981.